Moose

or
How I Learned
to Stop Worrying
and Love
My Broadway
Bomb

Arthur Bicknell

Acknowledgments

Thanks to all those who trod
the slippery boards of the Eugene O'Neill
with me thirty years ago.
Even more thanks to all the remarkable friends
and family members who have taken such good care
of me in the aftermath. And the greatest thanks
of all to the *Moose Murdered* production team
(Marsha Cohen, Laura Shelley, and
Barbara Koppelman), to my agent, Janet Rosen,
my revivalist, John Borek,
and especially to my editor
and "significant otter," Rachel Hockett.
Group Moose Hug!

This one's for me.

Prologue:

Moose, Now and Forever

I was sent to the principal's office for writing my first play.

It was a two-page allegory called *The Train Ride to Hell*, and was narrated by the devil, who, despite using words like "damn" and "penis," actually turned out to be the hero of the piece. I don't think the concept of the *antihero* was around in those days—not in the fifth grade, anyway—and besides, the teacher who found this opus stuffed in the back of my desk already had it in for me, for talking and—worse, *giggling*— during a group sing-along of "The Star Spangled Banner" some weeks earlier. The way she saw it, I'd already shown noisy disrespect for my country, and now here I was eulogizing Satan, for the love of God.

It was 1962 and even in the relatively progressive upstate New York public school system this kind of blasphemy was severely frowned on. It was obvious to my teacher that steps had to be taken—and fast.

The sad truth was that I was too big a wimp to be an effective rabble-rouser, and normally tried as hard as I could to follow all the rules. And it didn't matter who set down those rules, either. If something even *sounded* like a rule, no matter where it came from, you could count on me to do my very best not to break it. So this long walk down the hall to Mrs. Gelder's office was truly devastating, and I was shaking and sobbing uncontrollably by the time I got there.

Luckily, Principal Gelder knew exactly how I could make amends.

"Here's an idea. Why don't you write about *God*?" she said.

Grateful to be offered such an easy solution, I did exactly as she told me and handed in a new play—*The Train Ride to Heaven*—the very next morning. Not only was Mrs. Gelder appeased, but she proudly read my revision over the school's public address system. Before long, all the kids were submitting their own works to be read on the air, and Mrs. Gelder rewarded me by letting me host a new daily broadcast of cheerfully reverent student compositions.

At the tender age of eleven, I now knew all I'd ever have to know about the Game of Redemption.

But the real test of this knowledge didn't come along until twenty-one years later, when another one of my plays, receiving the worst reviews one could possibly imagine, opened and closed on Broadway on the same disastrous night.

A play I called *Moose Murders*.

Not even Mrs. Gelder could bail me out this time.

At first I decided the best laid plan for Moose *and* man would be to take it all on the chin and to remain unflappable for as long as it took to become unfloppable. I suspect I was still acting on that piece of advice from Mrs. Gelder—"write about God"—when I became determined to follow-up with some immaculate, relevant, and non-*farcical* drama which I'd write, naturally, under an assumed name (since my own was no longer of any use to anyone). Everything else would fall into place after that. Eventually I would nab the Tony nomination and the win, deliver a few deceptively eloquent words to my fellow "classmates," and then—just before the orchestra drowned me out—renounce my alias and reveal my antlers for the world to see.

"Hello, suckers! My name is Arthur, and I wrote *Moose Murders*."

Cue the falling chandelier.

Yeah, I was the Phantom; that's the best way I can describe my self-image during that fallout period right after the Moose detonated. I might be disfigured and scorned, sure, but I was at least willing to hole up in the bowels of the Paris Opera House (okay, a tiny apartment on Fourth Avenue and Tenth Street, but you get where I'm going with this) until coming up with some masterpiece so universally acceptable that I'd be able to peel off the porcelain mask, climb out of the shadows, and once again walk among theatergoers and critics alike. Plays come and go, I told myself, and even one this monumentally awful would eventually be forgotten.

I clung to that conviction for a very long time.

Months.

Years, even.

Eventually I stopped trying to "write about God," and embraced my inalienable right to relative obscurity. I'm happy to report that I've since reclaimed the use of my name and seldom feel the need any more to role-play as the Phantom of the opera.

That bad play of mine, however, went careening off in another direction beyond my control—or anybody else's. After a quarter of a century it's clear that the Moose has far outdistanced the man. It is legend. And it is that very phenomenon—the unwillingness of *Moose Murders* just to lie down and die the way it was supposed to—that many theater enthusiasts (including me) are still trying to figure out.

The element of *Moose Murders* I'd always been most confident about was its title. I thought it was memorable and silly and would have real staying power.

Got *that* right, at least.

While the effrontery of its opening-slash-closing night was still fresh in the minds of the estimated 1,150 witnesses to what the *New York Times* referred to as "one of the most magically dreadful nights in New York stage history," it wasn't surprising to see critics conjure up its name to ward off other artistically challenged productions following immediately in its wake. But the comparisons kept on coming year after year, and, to this day, *Moose Murders* stubbornly refuses to relinquish its status as *the* iconic Broadway disaster:

"Only the absence of antlers," wrote *New York Times* critic Frank Rich in 1988, "separates the pig murders of *Carrie* from the *Moose Murders* of Broadway lore." (Rich, in fact, has continued his love/hate affair with the Moose throughout his stint at the *Times* and beyond, every so often reaffirming the fact that it remained the worst play he'd ever seen, but that it did "remind one, however backhandedly, of the particular excitement of witnessing live theater.")

In November 2003, Michael Riedel of the *New York Post* reported that the production staff of the Farrah Fawcett vehicle *Bobbi Boland* "invoked two words to convince producer Joyce Johnson to close her show in previews: 'Moose Murders.'"

Again in the *Post* the following year, Clive Barnes proclaimed in his review of *Prymate*: "There have been worse plays on Broadway—*Moose Murders* comes to mind, and something about 35 years ago called *Fire*. Or perhaps it was *Fever*. Whatever."

The restless Moose hasn't confined itself to the theater. Throughout the years, misguided efforts in just about every branch of the performing arts have fallen prey to its legacy of ineptitude. In a 1989 classical music review for the *Washington Times,* after calling Kiri Te Kanawa's operatic treatment of *West Side Story* on Deutsche Grammophon "the decade's best unintentional comedy album," Octavio Roca went on to define *Utamaro* (the title of the Kennedy Center's production of Japan's first Broadway-style musical) as "Japanese for *Moose Murders.*"

About the 1998 debut of NBC's *Encore! Encore!* starring Nathan Lane, the *New York Observer* wrote: "It's the *Moose Murders* of sitcoms—it won't be here past Halloween, but the recollection of its awfulness will give you untold delight for years to come."

In 2001, the *New York Times* readied audiences for an American Ballet Theater premiere by announcing, "The suspense is about to end. Will (David) Parsons's new Pied Piper be ballet's answer to the wildly successful *Producers* or to the famously ill-fated *Moose Murders?*"

Not even the culinary world has been safe, as evidenced by Douglas Hunt's 1998 restaurant review in the *New York Law Journal*: "Mr. (Dean) Willis was the victim of one of the most capricious shut-downs in recent New York restaurant history earlier this year when the owners of the Garrick in the theater district pulled the plug on him nearly as fast as you can say mulligatawny. His run was slightly longer than *Moose Murders,* but not by much."

So what's in a name? Would things have gone differently if I'd called my play *Epic Proportions* or *Dance of the Vampires*? Would I be spared the constant barrage of snide references if I'd hit and run with some bland title like *Total Abandon* or *Rose's Dilemma*?

That rationale may have worked for the first few years of my denial, but having now forged well ahead into a new millennium, it's time to face up to the fact that there was a lot more than just a "catchy" title to set this bad boy apart from other legendary flops. Frank Rich caught on before anybody:

"From now on," he wrote in his now famous review of the show, "there will always be two groups of theater-goers in this world: those who have seen *Moose Murders,* and those who have not. Those of us who have witnessed the play that opened last night will undoubtedly hold periodic reunions, in the noble tradition of survivors of the *Titanic.* Tears and booze will flow in equal measure, and there will be a prize awarded to the bearer of the most outstanding antlers."

For weeks I regularly received notification from friends and family members of just about any reference the press made to my Broadway bomb. A lot of folks presumably felt strongly that I would never tire of seeing the name of my play in print, no matter what the context. Sometimes personal notes would be scribbled in the margins of the clippings they sent me, ranging from "damn the critics!" (an oath I found strangely unsatisfying) to "well, you never wanted to be a writer anyway" (so thoroughly insensitive it cheered me up a little). There were also those (a few remaining even today) who continued to give me the benefit of the considerable doubt, by holding on to the notion that I'd one day want to chronicle all this information for the official Moose Memoir.

You know, after I'd written a couple of critical and box-office hits, and could safely relegate *Moose Murders* to an anecdotal sidebar in a breezy piece for *Vanity Fair*.

While witnessing the legend of *Moose Murders* becoming an indelible part of Broadway lore, every so often I've been inspired to capitalize on its dubious notoriety. I've considered fictionalizing my experiences in another play or maybe even a novel—a scathing *roman à clef* filled with loosely disguised real-life luminaries, each one responsible in his or her own way for delivering the mortal blow to an already dying Broadway season. The major problem with this approach was that—aside from our original above-the-title star Eve Arden—there was nary a luminary to be found twinkling anywhere in the *Moose Murders* firmament. Most of us were rank amateurs, and what, I asked myself, would be the point of disguising any of us—loosely or otherwise—in a great, big, Broadway tell-all?

It just wasn't *Valley of the Dolls* material, and I had to live with that.

Another option—the one you're reading now—was to tell the real story to the best (or worst) of my memory. This was daunting at first because I honestly didn't want to offend or embarrass one living soul connected with the production—regardless of the degree of culpability I personally assigned to any of them individually. More to the point, no matter how disarmingly self-effacing I may have appeared immediately after the show's closing, I sure as hell wasn't ready to jump on the bandwagon by truly blaming *myself* for any of this mess.

As much as I'd like to elevate myself by saying so, back then, I was definitely *not* my own worst critic. Believe me, that distinction has taken time, practice, and unwavering commitment.

Happily, though, one of the perks of prolonged public ignominy has been learning to take myself—and everybody else—a lot less seriously. And, after twenty-six years, I think it's safe to assume that all the players in the *Moose Murders* saga have managed to move on, one way (Holland Taylor: Emmy Award for *The Practice*, 1999) or another (Eve Arden: R.I.P., 1990).

With all my favorite excuses dashed against the rocks, and with the serendipitous and rather mysterious recent reappearance of my journals from this period of my life, I'm ready now to name names and risk offending any of the poor souls who climbed aboard my vanity bandwagon as it sped toward the inevitable brick wall. I'm still concerned about tearing open old wounds, but have resigned myself to the fact there will always be at least one person in every room I enter who wants to know all the bloody details of my public execution, and probably even more who want to know just exactly how a play like *Moose Murders* winds up on Broadway in the first place.

So, slip on your commemorative antlers and pour yourselves a nice frothy glass of schadenfreude. Here's the story I'm sticking you with, boys and girls, straight from the Moose's mouth.

Oh, and belated thanks to you, Principal Gelder, wherever you are. I hope the journey was pleasant, whichever train ride you ended up taking.

Chapter One:

Our Miss Brooks

The three planned events of my first ever trip to Hollywood in December 1982 were visits to Disneyland, Universal Studios, and to the home of a movie star. For various reasons, all three were busts—but at least Eve Arden didn't charge admission.

John Roach, the producer/director of *Moose Murders*, had flown out to meet Eve a couple weeks before. He had been prepared to tackle certain "issues" the newly signed star had indicated she had about the script and the production that was slated to go into rehearsals in January for an early February opening (two days after my thirty-second birthday). Much to his relief, Eve never got around to talking shop, opting instead to show John and his wife Lillie Robertson slides of a recent trip she'd made to China. John was worried that I, as the playwright, wouldn't get off so easily, but frankly, I was looking forward to kicking back with the star of *Mildred Pierce*, and was more than ready to answer any question she might throw at me. I'd dealt with actors curious about the "history" or "motivation" of their characters many times before, and knew if I got backed into a corner I could always make up stuff on the spot. That's one of the advantages of being the "writer."

Besides, I was accompanied by my live-in accomplice Dennis Florzak, who was then also acting as my agent. I could always defer to him, especially if any of the questions required any left brain activity.

I called the Arden home from a payphone somewhere in Beverly Hills. Whoever answered sounded like Tweety Bird's "Granny" from the old *Looney Tunes*, and I figured this must be Eve's housekeeper or some other member of her staff assigned to answering phone calls. I introduced myself and asked if I might please speak with Miss Arden. In a split second, "Granny" disappeared, and the unmistakable resonance and staccato delivery of Connie Brooks declared "This *is* Eve Arden."

This was the first time I witnessed for myself Eve's uncanny talent as a quick-change vocal artist. I'd learn soon enough that the physical transformation into Eve Arden took a lot longer, requiring the services of manicurists, hair, wig, and turban stylists, and wardrobe consultants, among others. But when she needed to, Eve could modulate the timbre of her voice at the speed of a wisecrack—and drop about twenty years in the process.

We set up an appointment for later that afternoon. "I have some ideas," she said. "But, of course, every actress has ideas."

"I can't wait to hear 'em!" I chirped, and I really wasn't lying.

A few hours later, Dennis and I parked our rented Lincoln on a narrow street lined with terra cotta-shingled homes, and carefully began to make our way down a hill thick with exotic plants and shrubbery. Just before we reached the front door, we were intercepted by a short middle-aged man with slicked-back hair who introduced himself as Glenn, "Miss Arden's manager-of-many-years." We got the distinct impression this little guy had been hiding in wait behind a rubber tree plant for hours.

Glenn led us straight into the foyer of Eve's bungalow, where we were greeted by a dapper elderly man with a paisley ascot neatly tucked inside the collar of his short-sleeved shirt. I'd never met anybody who actually wore an ascot before. He reminded me of Vincent Price in one of those creepy and lush Roger Corman films of the 60s like *Masque of the Red Death*, and I remember thinking that he and the Peter Lorre look-alike Glenn were straight out of the pages of the old *Famous Monsters of Filmland* fan magazines. "Vincent" revealed himself to be Eve's husband, the actor Brooks West (was getting to rename your husband after the character you played on TV one of Hollywood's perks?), who invited us to follow him into the parlor where his wife would be joining us shortly.

The four of us sat down in a room filled with Chinese landscape paintings and dragon-handled vases and lamps, and chatted about *Anatomy of a Murder*, the film in which Brooks and Eve had appeared together in 1959. Suddenly, Glenn shot up off the couch and scurried over to the open French doors leading onto the terrace. A second later Eve made her entrance, her arms laden with snapdragons presumably freshly pulled from her garden. She was dressed as an equestrian, with a white hunt blouse, khaki jodhpurs, and Isotoner driving gloves.

Yoicks!

And talk about a towering presence. I'm six-foot-four myself, so height rarely impresses me. Maybe it was the light, or the fact that Glenn barely came up to her shoulders, but I thought Eve Arden was the tallest woman I'd ever seen in my life.

It looked like the casting people back in New York hadn't misled us when they originally pitched Eve for the lead role in *Moose Murders* by assuring us that she was still the "Our Miss Brooks" we all remembered from the popular sitcom of the 50s. She didn't look anywhere near her real age of seventy-four—which was a relief, since she was to play (among other things) the mother of a twelve-year-old girl and the secret lover of her thirty-something son-in-law.

After a brief tour of the garden, we all returned to the parlor. Eve directed Dennis and me toward a couch, and seated herself in the middle of a larger couch on the opposite side of the room. Brooks and Glenn then sat down in tandem, on either side of Eve.

We sat awkwardly smiling at one another until Eve finally broke the silence.

"You know," she said, "I wasn't sure this was right for me. But Brooks and Glenn tell me it's a very funny play and that I'll have fun."

"You think it's funny, *too*," said Brooks as he gently elbowed Eve in the ribs.

"Why, yes!" said Eve, pretending to scowl at her husband, and then setting us all at ease with a hearty three-note laugh.

"Ha, ha, ha!"

She held a beat and then cautioned: "but as I mentioned on the phone, we do have a few...ideas."

Taking his cue, Brooks grabbed a pair of reading glasses from an end table and handed them over to his wife. At the same time, a woman we hadn't met entered from the back of the house wheeling a tea wagon which she parked directly in front of Eve. This unidentified woman then immediately left the way she'd come, and we never saw her again.

There wasn't any tea or coffee on the tea wagon. Instead, there was a loosely-bound copy of *Moose Murders* crammed with dozens of post-it notes in a variety of colors. It looked like we were in for a long afternoon.

Eve adjusted her glasses and opened the script to the first bookmarked page. "Ah, yes," she said. "Stinky."

I could feel myself blushing. The character "Stinky" was the teenage son of Hedda Holloway, the starring role Eve would be playing. Essentially a 60s throw-back, Stinky was a smarmy pothead who had the hots for his mother. The script was full of his blatant sexual innuendos and tasteless bits of stage business. I wasn't surprised that this was where we'd begin our discussion.

"The three of us," Eve explained, "feel that 'Stinky' is inappropriate."

"Oh, God," I thought. "She doesn't just want to clean up his act, she wants to cut him out of the play altogether."

"We think 'Icky' might be more suitable."

"Oh," I said, caught completely off guard. "Why?"

Eve raised her eyebrows all the way to the top of her head, as if I'd just dropped my trousers and taken a piss in one of her dragon vases.

"For one thing," she said, "we saw *Sophie's Choice* the other night. Did you know there's a character named 'Stinky' in this movie? It's very popular and getting lots of exposure. People may feel the name's already been used."

What I *thought* at this moment was that, yeah, and Ibsen had "used" the name Hedda, and Fanny Brice had "used" the name *Snooks* (another character in *Moose Murders*), so what exactly is the point, here, but what I *said* was: "I think his name is '*Stingo*.'"

Eve stared at me with a perfect absence of expression.

"You know," piped in Glenn, "I think he's right. *Stingo* sounds right."

"What's more," said Eve, ignoring Glenn for the moment, "at the end of the play when my son-in-law Nelson asks me for Icky's real name, and I answer…" (she paused here to check her notes) . . . "'Damned if I know'— we thought that I could say 'He was named after his uncle Ichabod!'"

Johnny Carson once said in an interview that the best comeback line to use in situations like this is "you may be right." That way you manage to assuage your antagonist without actually conceding anything. Unfortunately, I didn't see this interview until many years later. Despite the apparent fact that Eve had no problem whatsoever being mauled, fondled, and groped by her drug-crazed eighteen-year-old son, and that all she really wanted me to do was to change his damn name, I, Playwright, presumed to lecture this venerable comedienne on the fragile nature of comedy.

As my voice gradually rose an octave, I explained to the triumvirate on the Big Couch that the line 'Damned if I know,'—although not exactly what any of us could call a real ripsnorter—was still probably a little more *unexpected*, a little less contrived, and therefore just a little *funnier* than "He was named after his uncle Ichabod!"

When I'd finished, Eve lowered her glasses and looked straight at Dennis, who may very well have said something to the effect of "you may be right"—whatever it was, it worked, and Eve turned to the next book-marked page of the script and read aloud:

"'I want to get into your pants, angel puss.'"

She waited for me to say something, but I was still cooling off from the last scrimmage.

"I don't think I'd say that line," she said.

"That's usually something a man says to a woman, isn't it?" said Brooks.

"But I *do* think I should wear pants—at least in the second act," Eve said. "I just don't know if they should be leather pants."

"Maybe a leather vest," said Brooks.

"Yes," said Eve, "a leather vest. And if it's only a vest, there's no need for me to say 'I've got more leather finery upstairs.' Because I don't think I'd say that line, either."

There were lots more lines she didn't think she'd say, and we proceeded to slog through them all, one by one. Unfamiliar with Old Hollywood proto-col, it took me a while to realize that the "she" who wouldn't say these lines wasn't so much Hedda, the character, as she was Eve Arden, the commod-ity. So I politely acquiesced a little, and just as politely (in my mind) held my ground a little, as Eve's frustration increased—along with the number of times she lowered her glasses and smiled imploringly at Dennis.

Without saying a word, Dennis was managing to bond with Eve very nicely.

She threw me a curve every so often by asking about something that had nothing to do with Hedda's dialogue. As planned, Dennis answered the more demanding (and far less interesting) questions, and I helped out wherever I could, fibbing as little as possible. There were some questions that neither of us knew how to answer—like "how will the rain storm be handled?" and "exactly *where* do I get stabbed?" and "how will the harness for Snooks be made?"—and we had to ask her to bring all these up with John once we got into production.

"Oh, Christ!" she said, after I'd passed the buck about what part of her body would be attacked by a butcher knife. My heart sank for a second until I realized she'd gone back to her list of lines she didn't think she'd say. "Oh, Christ!" was Hedda's last line before the first act curtain.

Thank God—only one more act to go.

"That could offend some people, although I myself say it all the time," said Eve.

"Oh, yes!" said Brooks, laughing.

"Nooo!" said Glenn, unintentionally (as far as I know) imitating Floyd the Barber from *Mayberry RFD*.

"But I think it would work better were I to say 'Oh, shit!' instead."

By this time Eve and I had come to an understanding of sorts. I had learned not to ask why, and she had learned that most of my script was etched in stone.

"You see," she said, "it's taken me several years to bring myself to the point where I can say 'Oh, shit!'—and I think my fans would get a kick out of hearing me say it. It would be something...*unexpected*." She smiled at me sweetly. "And I believe you were educating us a little while ago on just how funny that can be!"

By so neatly helping me hoist myself on my own comedy petard, Eve won this one hands down. In full view of the others, I wrote "Oh, shit!" in big red letters on my note pad.

Eve pretended to wipe away sweat, and then dramatically closed her *Moose* tome. "Well," she said, "I think we should quit while we're ahead."

"You mean while *you're* ahead," teased Brooks. (I was beginning to really like Brooks.)

Eve did a classic double take and then playfully poked her husband.

"Ha, ha, ha!"

She quickly got serious again. "We can take this all up again with John in New York," she said.

"We did want to talk a little bit about publicity," said Glenn.

"We covered all that with John, didn't we?" said Eve.

I was to learn later that certain rules regarding Eve's press during her six-month commitment to the play had indeed already been discussed with John, including the stipulation that we would all do our best to avoid mentioning any portion of the star's career prior to her Academy Award-nominated performance as Ida in the 1945 Joan Crawford vehicle *Mildred Pierce*. That meant, among other things, that we were not allowed to talk about her stint as a sketch artist in the Billie Burke and Shubert revival of *The Ziegfeld Follies* in the midthirties, or the 1937 film *Stage Door* in which she originated her signature role as the fast-talking, wisecracking sidekick. We could, however, freely talk to anybody about her most recent appearances as Principal McGee in the films *Grease* and *Grease 2*.

I also learned later that Eve had a solid tradition of secrecy regarding her real age, which explained her reluctance to have the press refer to her as a former Ziegfeld Girl. I never fully understood what all the fuss was about—as far as I was concerned she looked and sounded great, however old she was. Sure, if you put your nose right up to her ears you might be able to catch a glimpse of a little rough tissue, but I rarely had the occasion (or inclination) to be that intimate.

"I'm a little worried about candid rehearsal shots,"Eve confessed."Are we going to have to use a burlap scrim?"

"We understand,"I said."And we're all going to be very protective."

Dennis told me later that had we been offered any coffee, he probably would have done a spit take after I'd made this lofty remark. He was sure Eve agreed with him that the mere notion that somebody like *me* could ever manage to successfully protect somebody like *her* sped right past presumption and crashed straight into blind narcissism.

But my biggest faux pas of the afternoon, as it turned out, came after the"business"part of our meeting, when it looked like we were all free to indulge in some small talk before officially calling it a day. Brooks brought up *Anatomy of a Murder* again, and Eve told a story about her good friend Benay Venuta, a former vaudeville and musical comedy star I was personally unfamiliar with. (Although I loved the name"Benay"—especially the languorous way Eve pronounced it:"Buh naaaaay.")

As much as I was enjoying listening to Eve say the name "Benay," I was itching for some gossip about somebody I had actually heard of. I could tell both she and Brooks were getting ready to wrap things up, so I had to make a quick decision. Which of the dozens of stage and screen legends Eve had worked with throughout her career would I"casually"ask about? Jimmy Stewart? Robert Preston? Doris Day?

I decided to go for broke.

"Before we go," I said, "you *have* to give us the scoop on Joan Crawford! Was she really the *monster* everybody says she was?"

Eve heaved a big sigh, and shook her head sadly. "I have nothing negative to say about Joan," she said. "I think all this recent trash talk is undeserved. She was always very supportive, and she was absolutely instrumental in helping us with our first adoption. We couldn't have done it without her." (Eve and Brooks had four children, three of whom they'd adopted.)

My barefaced attempt to dish the dirt had obviously offended Eve deeply, so I tried to make it seem as though I'd only asked about Joan Crawford because of her indirect connection to one of the cast members of *Moose Murders.* The role of Eve's twelve-year-old daughter, Gay, had been given to Mara Hobel, the little girl who'd portrayed the young Christina Crawford in the film *Mommie Dearest* a couple years back. I asked Eve how she felt about that.

"I'm sure the press will have a field day." she scowled.

"We hear you've just come back from China," interrupted Dennis. "That must have been exciting."

Good save!

Once again in our comfort zones, we had a pleasant chat about the various pitfalls of traveling through foreign territory. Should Dennis and I ever decide to take on such an adventure, Eve strongly recommended that we take along a good supply of Ritz crackers.

"You never know how long you'll be stuck on a train," she said, "or exactly what you're going to find at the end of the track."

Good advice for us all.

Strongly sensing that we weren't quite ready to exchange warm hugs and kisses, I reverently shook Eve's gloved hand and wished her a merry Christmas while Brooks escorted us to the door.

"See you in New York," he called out, as we climbed back up the hill toward the car. "Let's hope we're all in for a happy New Year."

He waved cordially as we pulled away, reminding me once again of Vincent Price—this time in *The Fall of the House of Usher*. I half expected the Arden estate to explode and burst into flames behind him.

"So," I said to Dennis, "how do you think it went?"

"I'd say you probably blew it," he said.

"What do you mean? What did I do wrong?"

"You fought her over every point."

"I did not! I gave in to lots of things."

"Not without an argument."

"I was just *discussing*."

"You were *arguing*. She was very frustrated. You wore her out."

"What should I have done? Just taken my orders like a good little soldier?"

"You bet. For now, anyway."

"Well, that's ridiculous. Look, I respect the fact that she's a great Hollywood star, but I'm—"

"Nobody. You're absolutely *nobody* to her. She's got to get to know you, and trust you—and that's not going to happen if you don't at least *pretend* to let her have her way every once in a while. If you don't, you're going to force her to ignore you completely and to go to John for everything she wants."

"That might not be such a bad idea,"I grumbled.

"Yeah, we'll see how John reacts to *that*,"said Dennis.

As we made our escape out of the Hollywood Hills, the flames consuming the House of Arden burned red hot behind us.

We were to find out *exactly* how John would react to Eve's "ideas" sooner than we thought.

Chapter Two:

May the Force Be with You

Eve was by no means the first person approached to play the scheming matriarch Hedda Holloway in *Moose Murders*. More than a year before she finally took the bait—back when we were shooting for a spring 1982 opening—the well-respected casting team of Geoff Johnson and Vinnie Liff (along with their associate, Andy Zerman) had presented us with a list of potential Heddas that included the likes of Alexis Smith, Nancy Marchand, Geraldine Page, Beatrice Arthur, Jean Stapleton, Katherine Helmond, and Zoe Caldwell. One way or another (mostly through submissions to agents and managers), we'd been chasing after all of these ladies ever since—without much success. Eve herself, incidentally, never appeared on this or any subsequent list prepared by Johnson, Liff, or Zerman.

I'd actually written the role with Sada Thompson in mind, envisioning a hybrid of her bitterly malicious mother in the Off-Broadway production of *The Effect of Gamma Rays on Man-in-the-Moon Marigolds* and the wonderfully wise and nurturing mother she'd played in the mid-70s TV drama *Family*. Shortly before we acquired the services of Johnson-Liff, I had personally sent an unsolicited manuscript to Miss Thompson—something you're never supposed to do if you have no name recognition yourself.

She gave me a call anyway.

She told me the play was "laugh-out-loud funny," and that Hedda would be a "lark" to play.

"But the thing is," she said, "I'm too chicken to do this."

I asked her what parts of the script she found scary.

"No, it's not that," she said. "I don't know anything about the director. I've asked around, and nobody's been much help. I'll probably end up kicking myself, but I'm just too much of a coward to take the risk."

She didn't ask me about *my* credits, which was lucky because I doubt that my two previous, month-long Off-Off-Broadway showcases and one slightly longer limited run Off Broadway would have made much of an impression. I discovered in the months to come that my track record as a playwright rarely became an issue for actors presented with a script already optioned for Broadway. Somebody with big bucks had more or less validated it *and* me, so, for now, anyway, I wasn't that much of a liability.

Despite her apprehension about working with an unknown director, Sada didn't flatly turn down the possibility of doing the show, and asked me to keep her informed about its progress. Encouraged by this little ray of hope (and by the fact that she'd bothered to give me a call in the first place), I put a script in the mail to Anne Meara, who had seen and enjoyed my play *My Great Dead Sister*—a "coming-of-age" comic drama that had just about nothing in common with *Moose Murders*.

I knew Anne could easily take on the lead role of Hedda, but I thought she was much better suited to play the potty-mouthed Snooks Keene—a two-bit lounge singer who assumes the role of amateur detective to solve the mystery behind the play's rampant "Moose" murders. For what it was worth, Snooks and her blind husband Howie ("The Singing Keenes") were probably the most likable characters in the play. I thought if I could get Anne interested in playing Snooks, I might be able to get her to pitch the role of Howie to her husband, Jerry Stiller. "Stiller and Meara in *Moose Murders*" had a great ring to it.

Once Johnson-Liff Associates had been hired and had started sending out scripts, I decided to press my luck by giving Anne a call at home. Her charmingly effusive secretary Arnie put me right through.

"So, Arthur," said Anne. "What is it that you're doing with this thing called *Moose Murders*?"

"Believe it or not," I said, "it's going to Broadway! In April, if we can get it cast in time."

"You think it's right for Broadway?"

"Well, it's a big show."

"Yeah, and the 'bigger they are,' as they say. Anyway… who else is in the cast?"

"Well, nobody, right now, but Katherine Helmond seems interested."

"I love Kate! We debuted *The House of Blue Leaves* together twelve years or so ago, you know. Anybody else? How about the men? The blind guy and the lead—what's his name—Nelson?"

"Well, Paul Sand is looking at the role of Nelson, right now, and we're thinking about Richard Libertini for Howie, but—"

"Paul Sand's a doll. And I know Dick—he's a hoot."

"Yeah, but, I was thinking . . ."

"How about this 'Nurse Dagmar' character?"

"Carrie Nye is looking at that."

She was quiet for so long after that disclosure I thought I'd lost her.

"You know," she finally said, "I'm writing a play myself—because nobody else writes plays with parts in them for me."

"I did! It's called *Moose Murders*!"

"I'm going to hold you to that."

"Great! Wonderful!"

This conversation was going better than I'd expected.

"So, Arthur, is this going to Broadway?"

"Yes."

"Well, depending who's in it, I'd be interested."

"That's terrific!"

"Who's directing?"

"John Roach."

"Who's he?"

As with Sada Thompson, the old "Who's directing?" question proved to be a real conversation stopper. Things pretty much plummeted after that.

I'd already learned that you can squeak by with an unknown writer and even an unknown producer, but the relationship between an actor and a director is excruciatingly personal, and demands an enormous amount of trust. Outside the house of worship of your choice, it's next to impossible to find that kind of trust in the unknown. The more seasoned actors, who must now guard their hard-earned reputations with their lives, understand all too well that what they don't know may very well kill them.

There wasn't much information for Sada or Anne or anybody else to dig up about either the producer or the director of *Moose Murders*. They went by the respective names of Force Ten Productions, Inc., and John Roach, and they were one and the same.

As chief executive of Force Ten, John had dealt primarily with providing production services for feature and television films before shifting gears to tackle a Broadway production of *Moose Murders*. The company's biggest claim to fame to date was *Paradise Alley*, a movie written, directed, and starring Sylvester Stallone, about three Italian-American brothers living in the slums of New York in the 1940s.

John hadn't been happy about the way things turned out with this project. Just a few months after he and his business partner had optioned the *Paradise Alley* script (originally called *Hell's Kitchen*), Stallone had sold another one of his screenplays to the producer Irwin Winkler. Turns out this second screenplay—a little something called *Rocky*— mirrored the first to a large degree, prompting a legal battle that ended in a settlement out of court. Winkler and his associates then went on to produce Rocky in 1976, which made Stallone a star, won just about every award under the sun, launched a string of sequels, and pretty much overshadowed in every way possible the Force Ten production of *Paradise Alley* in 1978.

John had much higher hopes for the fate of *Moose Murders*.

It was while finishing his graduate studies at Pittsburgh's Carnegie Mellon University that John had met his bride-to-be, Lillie Robertson— the granddaughter of the "king of the wildcatters," Hugh Roy Cullen, one of Houston's most illustrious oil men and philanthropists. Aside from being John's spouse, it didn't appear that Lillie held any official position at Force Ten, but when I received my copy of the Moose Murders Limited Partnership prospectus in April 1982, I found her listed as a co-partner of two other companies that were part of the Moose conglomerate—"Force Nine" and "Force Nine Explorations Ltd," both based in Houston.

John was also chairman of the board, CEO, president, and principal patron of the Production Company, an Off-Broadway production house founded in 1977 by yet another Carnegie graduate, Norman René, who served as the company's artistic director until its closing in 1985. Norman, who died of complications from AIDS in 1996, was best known for his collaborations with writer Craig Lucas (including the stage and film versions of *Prelude to a Kiss*, and the groundbreaking 1990 film, *Longtime Companion*). I had the privilege of working with this engagingly demure and extraordinarily insightful man in 1978 when he directed his company's production of *My Great Dead Sister*, and again in 1980 when we moved this same play uptown for a longer run Off Broadway.

I handed a copy of my latest opus to Norman shortly after I'd pulled its final page out of the typewriter. Wisely foreseeing that this offbeat "mystery farce in two acts" would be too severe a departure from the Production Company's usual bill of faire, Norman, in turn, tossed the hot potato over to John Roach and Force Ten Productions, thereby setting in motion a chain of events that would make theatrical history.

That's right. It was all Norman's fault, and I'm happy to finally get that dirty little secret out in the open.

Based on the sketchy background I'd been given by Norman, I expected to find John swaggering around in a ten-gallon hat like J. R. Ewing, or to be covered in oil from head to foot, like James Dean in the movie *Giant*. So I was a little surprised when he turned out to be a young version of Bob Newhart, both physically and in his dry style of comic delivery. With his fashionable eyeglasses, his receding hairline, and his carefully sculpted beard and moustache, there was nothing remotely "rootin'" or "tootin'" about John Roach.

We hit it off right from the start—not just because we both got a kick out of my play, but because we instantly recognized each other for what we really were—two furtive hobgoblins masquerading as "nice guys." Soft-spoken and mild-mannered on the outside, we were both secretly harboring fierce vendettas against the human race. Perhaps as a direct result of this duplicity, we both thought sarcasm was grossly undervalued as a literary form, and were great fans of deep, dark, deadpan humor. We cringed at noisy outbursts, gravitating instead to "throw-away" remarks and barely audible barbs muttered under the breath. And yet we were remarkably well-behaved in public. We didn't like to rattle cages or rock boats—at least not while other people were looking.

Given this shared penchant for understatement, you might wonder why John and I so eagerly began to conjure up great plans for launching a play filled to capacity with tasteless sight gags, broad slapstick, and an assortment of garish characters, each one more loathsome than the last. I'd like to say our inner hobgoblins made us do it, but the real reason is far more convoluted.

This has always been the trickiest part of the whole Moose Capades to explain, so bear with me a minute. Like a lot of people I know, I've always loved the unintentional comedy that can come from a particularly bad play, movie, or TV show. Few things make me laugh harder than a really lousy performance delivered with irrepressible conviction. I'm also a sucker for inappropriately mundane or inappropriately profound dialogue inserted in the absolutely wrong place, and I have a fondness for painstakingly elaborate plot twists that lead nowhere. I wanted to write a play that would capture as many shades of this kind of, admittedly, *questionable* humor as possible, and thought the perfect venue for nonsense of this ilk would be a murder mystery. For the most part, the intentionally cheesy nature of the plot, characters, and dialogue of *Moose Murders* came across as intentionally funny on the page. I don't remember anyone ever reading the script and telling me "this is a *good* play," but just about everybody who read it said "this is a *funny* play." One of the main reasons John and I got along so well is because we both thought this kind of "bad" and "funny" would transfer easily onto the stage. In hindsight, I think our biggest downfall (if I had to pick *one*) was our tendency to equate "funny" with "good" in just about all aspects of our working relationship—especially in the beginning when there were plenty of easy laughs to egg us on.

When I first met John, he had recently purchased author John Hershey's old suite at the Dakota, the gargoyle-festooned building of countless legends, located on the corner of West 72nd Street and Central Park West. It was outside this building in December 1980 that Mark David Chapman had gunned down John Lennon. Lennon's wife, Yoko, and son, Sean, still lived here when John moved in, as did Leonard Bernstein and Lauren Bacall, among others. But what excited me more than anything else the first time I boarded the mahogany-paneled elevator that would take me to the headquarters of Force Ten, was that I was actually inside the "Bramford," the home of the fictional couple Rosemary and Guy Woodhouse from *Rosemary's Baby*, one of my favorite films.

This first summit meeting at the Dakota happened in late January of 1982, and had been called specifically to address a growing dissatisfaction with the lack of aggressiveness we all perceived to be coming from the Johnson-Liff Associates casting office. For several weeks, now, Geoff, Vinnie, and Andy had been chatting about the working habits of certain actors (so-and-so is always late to rehearsals; so-and-so is a notorious drunk, etc.), and endlessly discussing the relative merits of "ensemble" actors as compared to "percentage" and "name-above-the-title" actors—and yet not one actor of any category had signed on to the production of *Moose Murders*.

All the "forces-that-be" were in attendance for this meeting: John, Lillie, and vice president of Force Ten, associate producer of *Moose Murders*, and graduate of (you guessed it) Carnegie Mellon, Ricka Kanter Fisher.

Most people found Ricka Kanter Fisher to be as sharply intimidating as her three-pronged name. She had a strong jaw, a razor-edged tongue, and an eaglelike gaze that could penetrate steel. Everything about her was intense, including her sense of humor and her sense of loyalty. I liked her a lot.

"I'm sick and tired of the way they just humor us," said Ricka, referring to Johnson, Liff, and Zerman.

"When I *tell* them to do something, they'll go ahead and do it," said John. "But that's not enough."

"We need them to take some initiative," insisted Lillie, whom I was meeting for the first time this afternoon.

Unlike her husband, Lillie could be very outspoken—but this was something I wouldn't really see for myself until we were much further along into the production. For now, all I saw was an uncommon blend of poise and vitality that came very close to matching my mental image of what a real Houstonian should look like. She had the kind of physical beauty that sends men off to their garrets to write pages and pages of gushy poetry. It was as if she'd stepped out of a Victorian cameo broach, thrown on a pair of designer jeans, and gone outside just long enough to let the sun burn off all that ivory veneer. And yet she somehow managed to completely retract her "larger-than-life" persona at will—so convincingly, in fact, that (warning—spoiler ahead) when future casting director Stuart Howard had first visited the Force Ten headquarters, he mistook her for "the maid."

"They can't get a handle on any of the five lead characters—not Hedda, or Snooks, or Howie, or Dagmar or Nelson," continued John, "let alone Joe Buffalo Dance, Stinky, or Gay."

"Or Lauraine," I said, referring to Hedda's mousy and neurotic oldest daughter—one of my favorite characters.

John sank back into his chair and delicately coughed up a little phlegm.

"No," he finally said. "Lillie's playing Lauraine."

"Oh," I said. "I didn't know that."

"Really? Wow. I guess in my mind I'd already discussed it with you. Sorry."

"Would anyone care for some sparkling water?" asked Lillie.

Dennis later suggested that this would have been the perfect time for me to say "Well, in *my* mind Dennis is playing Nelson."

What burned my ass was not so much that Lillie was going to play Lauraine (although I had a hunch we could find any number of less spectacularly beautiful candidates for the role out there somewhere), but that I, the father of the Moose, was apparently the last one to know about this nuptial agreement.

Some time before John rolled this little grenade under my chair, Ricka had made arrangements for Force Ten Productions to meet with Vinnie and Andy later that afternoon. The rest of us, now walking on eggshells and exercising round-shouldered civility, might never have found the collective spines to venture out of the Dakota onto the mean streets below had Ricka not continued to take charge. She practically buttoned our coats before leading us out the door to take care of business. It was quite obvious where the "force" in Force Ten Productions came from.

To our chagrin, Geoff and Andy weren't particularly apologetic about the lack of progress with the casting for *Moose Murders*. As if speaking to very slow children, they explained to us that this was par for the course for most productions. "We spent two years trying to cast *Solomon's Child*," Geoff said, "intending to secure Dustin Hoffman or Al Pacino. We ended up with John McMartin. That's the way it goes."

"But McMartin was good. He was really *good*," Andy was quick to add.

"Please tell us exactly where things stand right now," demanded Ricka.

We were then given updates of the status of just about every actor who'd been approached to join the cast of *Moose Murders*. Alexis Smith was a definite "no," no explanation offered. Zoe Caldwell's production of *Medea* at the Kennedy Center in April would be moved to Broadway later in the season, so count her out, as well. There was chatter about a possible eleventh season of *Mash* which, of course, would tie up David Ogden Stiers, but rumor also had it that the TV drama *Lou Grant* was on its last legs, so Nancy Marchand might very well be "looking" again. Both Katherine Helmond and Carrie Nye had responded favorably to the script, but both wanted information on the rest of the cast, and about the director.

"This 'director' issue is the biggest single concern for most of these folks," Geoff said, after he and Andy had exhausted their notes. "There's a lot of trepidation out there about unknown directors."

"Fine," said John, petulantly. "I don't mind trepidation, but it's not as if my direction comes as a surprise *string* attached at the last minute. And I don't appreciate all these 'no's' without any reasons—especially when they come right after initial consents."

"They just don't know your work," said Geoff.

"Well, that can be remedied. I'm directing a show at the Production Company at the beginning of March. But I'd rather not wait until then to see some results."

"Maybe we should explore soliciting some agent submissions here in New York," suggested Andy, "instead of going after glittering names from L.A."

"You told us originally that you wanted to take care of the *legends* first, before going after the others," reminded Geoff.

"Fine," said John. "Give me a list of 'real actors' from New York."

Leaving the Johnson-Liff office that afternoon, we all felt reasonably secure that our casting crisis was now under control. We all liked the idea of abandoning the movie-star wild Moose chase, and were eager to start hearing from all those great stage actors who, being so unconditionally committed to the vanishing art of live theater, wouldn't be so goddamn picky about technicalities like playwright, producer, director, and Lillie Robertson as "Lauraine."

When we were alone, I asked John how his investors would feel about "nonglitter."

"My investors," he said, "owe me favors. But I think I'd have a better chance of convincing them in the *next* tax year."

All was still deathly quiet on the casting front in March when the "remedy" John had proscribed for those unfamiliar with his work as a director—a play called *The Chinese Viewing Pavilion*—concluded its run at the Production Company. Mel Gussow of the *Times* was not kind to the playwright or cast members (Lillie was one of these), but was comparatively easy on John:

"John Roach's direction is listless."

Still, this wasn't exactly the kind of inspirational testimonial we were all hoping for.

After another few months went by with Lillie maintaining her status as the sole cast member of *Moose Murders*, it was looking as if John wouldn't have to worry about saddling his investors with any 1982 expenses. The initial spring production date turned into a late September opening, which, in turn, became Halloween. After that, Geoff suggested that we wait for the first "fall fiascos," and then move in to settle for a late winter/early spring 1983 opening. John conceded that this would be a "possibility." I kept waiting for the phone call from Ricka or John that would advise me that the project had been totally scrapped and that John had now decided to buy a football team instead.

During this time I kept in touch with Anne Meara fairly regularly. In June, John had me set up a meeting for the two of them, stressing that I was to tell Anne that he would be wearing his director's hat only. (He had by now handed over most production elements to Ricka and the show's general manager, Eddie Davis of Theatre Now, Inc.)

A few weeks after this meeting (which had gone well, according to John), Dennis and I ran into Anne at a bakery shop on West 57th street.

"Hey, Arthur! CBS is doing my movie!"

"Is this the play you were writing?"

"Nah, it's a whole different project. We're wrapping it up at the end of November, beginning of December. Locales in New England and Yonkers—all of 'em shot in L.A. What are you gonna do?"

"See," said Dennis. "She's available."

"So, Anne," I said, never one to ignore a cue to beat a dead moose, "is there a sparkle of interest left in *Moose Murders*?"

"Oh, yeah, the old 'Moose that Roared.' I'll tell you, Arthur, here's the thing. I think I'd feel guilty playing half a comedy team without Jerry."

"How would you feel about playing half a comedy team *with* Jerry?"

"Terrific."

"Well, I have my ways, you know."

"This Moose still headed for Broadway?"

"Yeah, we're targeting late winter or early spring now."

"Who's directing?"

"John Roach," I said calmly. "If I've said it once, I've said it a million times. You've talked to him on the phone. You visited his apartment about two weeks ago, and you had a lovely, lovely time." I grabbed hold of both her hands. "John Roach, John Roach, John Roach!"

"Oh, God," said Anne when I let her go. "You gotta forgive me. Do you know what it's like having had your last period six months ago?"

In early July, Johnson-Liff Associates terminated their contract with Force Ten Productions. They sent John a letter explaining that they felt they had "exhausted" their energies toward the *Moose Murders* project, and that a "fresh approach" was perhaps called for. They said they felt very bad that the show had not been cast by this date and told Force Ten to feel free to consult with them for any casting advice in the future.

John actually seemed blasé about this news. To tell the truth, I was a little relieved myself. I can't speak for the others, but the Johnson-Liff boys always made me feel as if I was sitting at the dweeb table at the school cafeteria. (Not that I wasn't used to that, but still.)

As coincidence would have it, Geoff, Vinnie, and Andy weren't the only ones to drop out of the picture in July. After meeting Anne at the bakery shop, I'd talked to John about offering Stiller and Meara the roles of "The Singing Keenes." I was quite willing to expand Howie's lines, to balance things out. John was all for it, and since we were currently without casting representation, he suggested that I call Anne to feel things out.

After a little small talk, Anne came right to the point.

"Arthur, I love you, and I love the play, but my priority is the CBS film."

"I bet we could work around the film."

"What can I tell you? I've also got a special for HBO with Jerry. But tell me something. Have you got a good director?"

"Yep. John Roach. I think I may have mentioned that already."

"Who?"

"Don't start with me, Anne. Just don't do it."

"Well, tell you what."

"What?"

"You let me know when your director drops dead, okay?"

This time I got the message.

"Bunch of dilettantes," snarled Dennis, obviously in need of having a thorn yanked from his paw.

It was the first week of August, and we were baking away in our tiny kilnlike apartment near Astor Place. The only word we'd heard from Force Ten Productions since the departure of Johnson-Liff Associates nearly a month ago was from Ricka, who called to see if I might be willing to coax Anne Meara to attend an upcoming fundraising event for the Production Company. I'd asked her how things were going with the show, and she'd told me that John had hoped Eddie Davis's Theatre Now would take on the job of casting, but that they unfortunately had no time to spare for us since becoming immersed in projects for NBC Entertainment. "So," she said, "we're back to square one."

"They'll lose interest altogether," Dennis predicted. "They'll find another lollipop in the candy store. No big deal. Just give the money back to the investors and write this particular endeavor off as a tax loss."

I tried to cheer us both up by rattling off all the feathers we'd managed to attach to our moose-hunting cap. Marjorie Bradley Kellogg had signed on as scenic designer. I remembered the magnificent set she'd designed for the recent George C. Scott revival of Coward's *Present Laughter* at the Circle in the Square. She'd also created the sets for the Broadway productions of

Steaming, Extremities, and *The Best Little Whorehouse in Texas,* so nobody could get away with calling this lady a dilettante.

Another gem, Betty Lee Hunt, had been hired as press representative. Betty's agency, Hunt/Pucci Associates, was currently handling *Torch Song Trilogy,* and also had the Broadway productions of *Agnes of God* and *Crimes of the Heart* under its belt. And the wonderfully demented cartoonist Gahan Wilson had agreed to do the graphics.

"And let's not forget," I said, "that the play has been capitalized for months. Months! Come on, how many starving playwrights get this kind of deal thrown in their laps?"

"In case you haven't noticed, you're still starving," said Dennis, who must have been getting awfully tired of wearing that hooded black robe and lugging a big old scythe around our tiny hot apartment.

This is as good a time as any to point out that Broadway was still considered to be the brass ring for many aspiring American playwrights back in the late 70s and early 80s. The British invasion headed by the likes of Cameron Macintosh and Andrew Lloyd Webber was only just beginning, the theater district had not yet been Disney-fied, and it would be years before out-of-control production costs and consequent out-of-control ticket prices forced producers to sink their money solely into bankable revivals of classic plays and musical adaptations of hit movies. Back then, there was still a slight chance that a new American play could open on Broadway and that people might actually be able to afford to see it.

But even then, the journey from the typewriter to the Great White Way did not, as a rule, happen overnight. More often than not, you would have to go through many drafts of your script before ever seeing any sort of fully realized stage production. There would be retreats to writers' colonies, showcases sometimes sponsored by Actors' Equity and sometimes not, staged readings held in somebody's basement, or wine and cheese backers' auditions held in somebody's Upper-East Side apartment—through all of which you would continue to rethink, reshape, and rewrite—and then rewrite some more. And even if you were lucky enough to find a producer willing to take a risk on your play, you could expect to go through many more drafts at some out-of-town regional theater before even *thinking* about taking your show to Broadway.

I'd gone through versions of this process with my two previous plays. Some critics had actually found nice things to say about these first efforts,

suggesting, a few of them, that I was a "playwright of promise." The shelf
life for this "promising" phase in the life of a playwright is rather nebulous,
but you stand a much better chance of breaking through to the next level
by arming yourself with feedback from smaller public forums before doing
battle in the Broadway coliseum.

Frank Rich put this all in perspective in an article for the *Times*
about four months after *Moose Murders* closed. "There were only three
new American plays produced expressly for Broadway this season, without prior stagings at institutional or regional theaters," he wrote. "One,
Brighton Beach Memoirs, was a fait accompli, given that its author is our
best known playwright; the other two were *Moose Murders*, and another,
equally junky one-night flop, *Total Abandon*." (More about *Total abandon*
later, by the way.)

Force Ten Productions had conveniently eliminated all such "institutional" steps for *Moose Murders*, sparing me the grueling development
process in its entirety. Sure, there had been some quibbling at first about
whether or not we'd take the show *straight* to Broadway—the original contract had, in fact, been for an Off-Broadway production. But for any number of financial reasons (none of which I ever bothered to ask about), it
wasn't long before a new contract had been made up and Force Ten had
posted the bond for a first class Broadway production.

Like a kid waiting for Christmas morning, I was too impatient to go
over the first and only draft of *Moose Murders* for any glaring errors in
character development or any gaping holes in its plot. Rather than using
this down time constructively, I spent hours daydreaming about quitting
my job as a reservationist for Air France, moving out of my cramped apartment, and finally paying back all the money I owed to various members
of my family. I may have managed to grab hold of the brass ring on the
merry-go-round, but it looked like my free ride had been postponed in-
definitely.

And then, in the dog days of summer, what to my wondering eyes
should appear but Stuart Howard and Amy Schecter of the Pulvino &
Howard casting office. Just hours after having received the script to *Moose
Murders*, Stuart had been on the phone with Ricka, exchanging favorite
lines from the play. He could barely contain himself, and his colleague
Amy was equally enthusiastic. I couldn't imagine a more dramatic contrast
to the cool reserve persistently maintained by the team of Johnson, Liff,

and Zerman. Stuart and Amy not only got the play, they got me—and neither one of them was the least bit averse to sitting right down with me at the dweeb table. My first meeting with them was the most fun I'd had since I'd gotten on board this carousel called *Moose Murders*, and I could tell immediately that these were the guys who were finally going to crank up its engine.

Chapter Three:

The Call of the Wild

In late September I sat in on an Equity Principal Interview for *Moose Murders*. Essentially cattle calls mandated by the union, these events took place over a designated period of time in grungy, harshly lit rooms adjacent to the lounge in the Actors' Equity building on West 46th Street. For any actor who'd been around the block more than once, an EPI held about as much appeal as an army physical.

It was common knowledge (at least in the days when the Moose was loose) that most shows heading for Broadway or Off Broadway had been precast long before these interviews were even announced. If by some fluke a role or two remained open, you still shouldn't get your hopes up because chances were great you'd be chatting with somebody on the bottom of the production's food chain whose opinion—good or bad—wouldn't count for much. So the best you might expect was to be put on a list as a possible understudy—and even that was a long shot.

Moose Murders, however, had not been precast (although God knows we'd tried), and despite the fact that we were still looking for "name" performers, most of the actors who bothered to show up for our EPIs had at least a fighting chance to be considered for just about any role in the play. Pulvino & Howard's Amy Schecter had drawn the short straw and was conducting the interviews the day I attended. She told me that she and Stuart had been deluged by submissions from agents, and had already filled every time slot for the regular audition period beginning October 7. Since submissions were still coming in, it was likely we'd be extending auditions throughout the month, in which case we'd also draw from a holding file of promising interview candidates.

If you had to subject yourself to an EPI, you couldn't have found a better person than Amy to see you through the ordeal. She was warm and down-to-earth with every single person who straggled in during the time I was there, putting everybody (including me) at ease immediately. This was especially helpful for this kind of nonaudition process, where there were no sides of the play's dialogue for actors to read from. Instead, they had to rely on making an impression with either the "right look" (whatever that might be) or with some kind of memorable small talk. That's about as daunting a situation as you'll find in the business.

Without having access to the script, the only guideline to what we were looking for was the cast breakdown that had appeared in the trade papers the week before:

> **Snooks Keene:** lead, 40–45, half of "The Singing Keenes," off-key and overly enthusiastic, tough, funny. Prototype—Anne Meara.
>
> **Howie Keene:** 40–45, Snooks's husband, sings OK, blind, preferably thin. Prototype—Dick Libertini.
>
> **Joe Buffalo Dance:** 50s, a mock American Indian, caretaker of the Wild Moose Lodge.
>
> **Nurse Dagmar:** lead, 30 and over, big, powerful, beautiful, gorgeous body, maybe exotic. Prototypes—Sally Kellerman or Rula Lenska.
>
> **Hedda Holloway:** lead, 50–55, impressive WASP matriarch, the "eye of the storm," always in control. Prototype—Sada Thompson.
>
> **Stinky Holloway:** 18–20, Hedda's son, quite a bit grotesque, "in lust" with his mother. Should be physically striking, could be chubby or very skinny.
>
> **Gay Holloway:** 12. CAST.
>
> **Lauraine Holloway Fay:** CAST
>
> **Nelson Fay:** CAST.

The male lead of Nelson was listed as "cast" because Jeffrey Jones (currently in the Off-Broadway ensemble of Caryl Churchill's wonderful play *Cloud Nine*) had tentatively committed to playing the part, and the role of Hedda's twelve-year-old daughter, Gay, called for little girls who could tap-dance, so we'd all decided we'd hold agent-exclusive auditions for these little darlings (and their stage mothers) at a later date. Lauraine, of course, had long since been claimed by Lillie.

I laughed out loud when I saw that Stuart had included Rula Lenska as a prototype for Nurse Dagmar. Rula had appeared in the British TV series

Rock Follies in the 70s, but here in America she was known primarily for a series of Alberto VO5 shampoo commercials which always began with a close-up of her announcing in a deep, husky voice "I'm Rula Lenska." All anybody really knew about her was that her name was "Rula Lenska" and that she apparently needed to keep her hair looking nice. When I'd thrown her name out as a possible Dagmar, Stuart had been the only person in the room to crack up (aside from me, of course). John and Ricka hadn't taken this suggestion seriously, especially since Equity was currently foaming at the mouth over an influx of British imports, but it was nice to see that Stuart was giving me an honorific wink and nudge.

It was interesting to see how broadly some actors interpreted descriptive phrases from the breakdown the likes of "overly enthusiastic" and "quite a bit grotesque," and I noticed that none of the suggested age ranges had made much of an impression. Most of the folks who came in were pleasant and perfunctory, acting as if they were here to pick up their dry cleaning. I realized soon enough that I wasn't going to get anything more out of this experience than they were, and, doing my best to keep a low profile (I was *not* a union cardholder), made my way back through the lounge to the elevators. Just in time, too, since I could tell the Equity officials were about ready to point and scream at me like the pod people in *Invasion of the Body Snatchers*.

The fog of ambivalence still hanging over me from the EPIs finally lifted a week later when I arrived at the Michael Bennett Studio on Broadway. The first thing I saw was a glass showcase in the lobby displaying the legend, "*Moose Murders*, Studio One."

"Holy shit," I thought. "It's real."

As soon as I entered the cavernous Studio One, Stuart came bounding over to me like an overgrown puppy, and vigorously shook my hand. He introduced me to Mary McTigue, a lean and angular young woman in a tweed suit who had been hired to read with the auditioners.

"I just *adore* your play!" said Mary with a thick nasal twang that reminded me of Gloria Upson, Patrick's gentrified fiancé from *Auntie Mame*.

Stuart then directed me to a seat next to John and Ricka at a long table near the front of the room. There was a place setting for each of us consisting of a freshly bound *Moose Murders* script, a note pad, a coffee mug and water glass, a pack of breath mints, and a copy of this morning's "program"—vital statistics concerning each of the actors we would soon be seeing. A huge stack of actors' resumes and head shots had been neatly positioned on the left side of the table.

"I love your caterer," I whispered to John.

"The mints are à la carte," he said.

Before long Amy entered from the hallway outside the studio to announce the arrival of our first appointment, the actor Richard B. Shull who would be reading for the role of Howie. Richard had a lived-in face that I recognized from dozens of films and TV commercials, and had completely memorized his audition piece—a nice stroke of professionalism that was seldom displayed by those to follow.

Next in was Lois Smith, the terrific actress who'd played any number of very serious roles in movies, including the concert pianist sister of Jack Nicholson in *Five Easy Pieces*. She looked disgruntled, as if she'd just caught whiff of some foul smell. Stuart introduced her to the "panel," and when she got to me she looked me straight in the eye and said acrimoniously: "This is a *very* silly play." She then gave us a Nurse Dagmar that could have come straight out of Brecht's *The Caucasian Chalk Circle*.

Michelle Shay, on the other hand, who'd just gotten raves as Titania in the Shakespeare in the Park production of *A Midsummer Night's Dream*, gave us a sultry and seductive Dagmar, whereas Judy Graubert from PBS's *The Electric Company* offered a wide-eyed and totally manic Dagmar that was actually just what I'd envisioned for the role of Lauraine.

I didn't know what to expect from Mink Stole, one of John Waters's discoveries and the star of his early classic underground films *Pink Flamingos* and *Female Trouble*, but I wouldn't have been surprised if she'd shown just the right sensibilities to knock Snooks out of the park. Unfortunately, Mink acted like she'd wandered into this building entirely by accident, and seemed bewildered when asked to read out loud from the script. Dana Ivey, at that time playing Monica in the Circle in the Square production of *Present Laughter*, fared much better with her sharp and tough Brooklynese version of Snooks.

The first one in after our lunch break was my older brother Bruce, an accomplished architect who'd worked out of Colorado and New Mexico for several years before falling onto some hard times. He was in his early fifties, and had recently pulled up stakes and moved east to make a fresh start of things here in New York. So far, not too many architectural opportunities had cropped up, but, on the brighter side, there had been lots of time to put his community theater skills to the test. With his Santa Claus-length snowy white beard and twinkling blue eyes, Bruce was causing a modest sensation in the Off-Off-Broadway community—some of the companies for which he'd worked had even been willing to spring for cab fare.

I don't think Bruce ever really expected to be cast in *Moose Murders*— he just needed to see for himself what the current fuss over his little brother was all about. He was convinced I'd fashioned the character of Joe Buffalo Dance after a man named Freddie Brack, the real-life caretaker of a lodge at Big Moose Lake in the Adirondacks next door to the camp our father had purchased in the thirties. Having known Freddie for years, it made perfect sense to Bruce that he should at least be considered to portray the man on stage, and that he might even bring the show a little authenticity.

"God, I was scared," he admitted to me on the phone that evening. "It was all so impressive. Are you sure I didn't embarrass you?"

"Of course not," I said, without flinching.

I didn't dare tell him that the formality of the audition process also impressed the hell out of me, and that I was struggling to maintain my own brittle sense of entitlement. This wantonly paranoid side of me suspected that Bruce's underlying motivation for showing up this afternoon might have been to somehow find a way to defraud me, and I was relieved to hear that the facade of the Michael Bennett Studio had managed to protect me so well. We hadn't grown up together (Bruce had moved out West to start his own career and family shortly after I was born), so this burgeoning sibling rivalry—whether real or imagined—was something strange and new that I wasn't at all sure how to handle with all the other strange and new things going on all around me.

Apparently I wasn't alone in my confusion. After my brother finished his very earnest, and, yes, *authentic* audition, a conversation gap threatened to suck all life from the room. "So," I said, to fill it, "I think my Aunt Betty is next. She's got her eye on the role of Hedda."

For the next hour or so, we watched our reader Mary McTigue play Hedda to a parade of Stinkys of all shapes and sizes, many of whom sought to disarm us with their improvisational comedy. Mary seemed unfazed when one actor suddenly fell to the floor and desperately entangled both his arms around her leg, but she did start to become unglued when her many polite attempts to dislodge him failed miserably and she was forced to drag him along with her on her escape route across the room. She came dangerously close to losing it when another Stinky snuck up behind her and planted a loud, sloppy raspberry on her neck. She finally had to request a five-minute break after one exceptionally bizarre young man spent his entire reading fixating on her bosom while methodically playing with himself (something, by the way, that's really difficult to do while also holding your book).

Mary wasn't the only one worn out by the end of the afternoon. Our circuits were overloaded and we were all bleary-eyed from watching what essentially amounted to an eight-hour, nonstop variety show. It was only the first day, and already we'd seen everything except the guy spinning plates on sticks while accompanied by Khachaturian's "Sabre Dance."

And then in walked June Gable with a full set of china.

She was wearing a fake leopard skin halter top, shocking pink skin-tight chinos and tacky gold "come-fuck-me" pumps. She'd teased her hair until it had unconditionally surrendered, and had thickened her lashes with enough mascara to offend Tammy Faye Baker. With just a little more taste and reserve, she might have been ready to reprise her role as bathhouse performer Googie Gomez in Terrence McNally's *The Ritz*.

She launched right into a swing version of "Jeepers Creepers," simultaneously pulling out every stop and slaughtering every note along the way. Halfway through the number, she ran over to the handbag that she'd left by the door and whipped out a pair of novelty glasses with droopy eye balls on springs. She put them on and flounced over to the table, letting her droopy eyes dangle in John's face and across his chest. "I just can't take my eyes off you," she said, then went back "upstage" to belt out her finale.

Way back when, Johnson and Liff had cautioned us about June Gable's penchant for scene stealing during Hal Prince's 1974 Broadway revival of *Candide*. She'd won a Tony nomination for her role as the Old Lady in that production, but had apparently pissed off a lot of her fellow actors with her total disregard for ensemble team work. When or if push came to shove, Geoff and Vinnie thought John might have considerable trouble reining her in.

But it was just this sort of excessive enthusiasm that defined the character of Snooks. June's lounge act was maybe a little too bad-Vegas as opposed to bad-Adirondacks in this first audition, but that was just a matter of fine tuning as far as we were concerned. She'd made us scream with laughter at the end of the day when our brains were fried and all we'd really wanted to do was to crawl home and fall into our beds. If she'd so easily managed to revive us, think of what she could do for all those bridge and tunnel crowd matinees. So what if she was guilty of a little upstaging every now and then?

If scenery be the food of laughter, chew on, June, chew on.

A large part of the second day of auditions was devoted to blatant cronyism. John had long since played the vanity card by anointing himself director and by casting his wife in the show, and I thought it was high time for me to start reaching into the cookie jar myself. It had always been my intention to finesse John into hiring Dennis as Nelson's understudy (the role itself was going either to Jeffrey Jones or some other "name" actor), but I couldn't really broach the subject as long as Dennis continued to act as my agent. The trick was to tie up all the loose ends of my contract with Force Ten in time for Dennis to "cut me loose" and ease into his new role as understudy. Once the show was on its feet and running, I figured it shouldn't be too hard to find myself another agent to take up the slack.

Yeah, I know. The operative word there was "running."

Once you'd eliminated all the lead roles earmarked for known actors and the one role precast, the pickings were pretty damn slim. You had eighteen-year-old Stinky, twelve-year-old Gay, the middle-aged caretaker that my brother had tried out for, and one other character with no lines who wasn't even mentioned in the cast breakdown, and yet was destined to be singled out by just about every theater critic as a prime example of the limitless depths into which *Moose Murders* plunged: Hedda's husband Sidney Holloway, a wheelchair-bound quadriplegic wrapped in bandages from head to toe.

Between us, John and I had a considerable number of college chums who were pursuing careers as professional actors, but most of these folks fell outside the age range of the available roles. A few of them, though, were physically and vocally flexible enough to understudy multiple roles (gaining a Broadway credit and an Equity scale paycheck in the process), so it wasn't long before a sort of collegiate "Sharks" and "Jets" gang warfare started to materialize.

John's Carnegie Mellon team consisted of Brad O'Hare, a young leading man I suspected was being groomed for the role of Nelson should Jeffrey Jones bail out, Anderson ("Andy") Matthews, a funny and very personable guy who reminded me of a young Buddy Hackett, and Suzanne

Henry, a talented singer who had costarred with Craig Lucas in the Stephen Sondheim revue *Marry Me a Little* when it debuted at the Production Company in 1981.

My own alma mater, Ithaca College, was represented by my roomie Dennis and two other close partners in crime: Marc Castle, the man to whom I'd dedicated *Moose Murders* and whose flawless portrayal of a nerdy fifteen-year-old in both incarnations of *My Great Dead Sister* had earned rave reviews (despite the fact he'd been pushing thirty at the time), and Jane Dentinger, the Dorothy Parker to my George S. Kaufman (in our own minds, anyway), and the lady who—possessing the barbed wit and quick delivery of Fran Lebowitz and the singing voice of Lucy Ricardo—had been the inspiration for the character of Snooks Keene.

When Jane stopped by the casting office to pick up her audition sides, the young man at the desk had urgently warned "you'd better do something to make yourself look older!" Under different circumstances, this might have been music to her ears. As it was, she told me later she had to stifle the urge to grab the kid by the collar and scream "Fuck you! I'm the prototype!"

Remembering that she had once lunched with Ann Miller, Marc suggested that Jane try to borrow one of the veteran hoofer's indestructible wigs for the upcoming audition—or, better yet, just snatch the current one off the old gal's head as she walked by. "She has so many," he said. "She'll never miss it." As viable an option as this was, Jane decided instead to shell out fifty bucks for a session with her mentor Larry Moss, an acclaimed acting coach then teaching in New York.

As soon as Jane walked into the studio that second afternoon, she and I took care of a little preplanned business. Oblivious to everybody else in the room, we exchanged a little banter from *Murder on Cue*—Jane's debut mystery novel that had been sold to Doubleday earlier that year and was due to be published shortly after the opening of *Moose Murders*. We both felt at that time that we'd *earned* the right to be so publicly precious, I suppose. The scene we enacted was a reunion between actress/amateur sleuth Jocelyn O'Rourke and playwright Austin Frost (I'd managed to talk her out of calling this guy "Arthur Bracknell"), on the occasion of Austin's illustrious return to Broadway. Whether life was imitating art or the other way around, Jane decided right then and there that in her next book, she would definitely have Jocelyn win a Tony Award.

She tore the room apart. I'd acted with her in a number of college and summer theater productions, and had seen her perform two of the three characters in the long-running Off-Broadway hit *Vanities*, but had never seen her pull off such a tour de force. My jaw would have dropped if I hadn't been laughing so hard. She made such an impression on Stuart that he demanded his own copy of her picture and resume for future reference, and was still singing her praises at the end of the afternoon.

"She must have experience with stand up comedy," he said. I told him I didn't think she had, and he looked at me if I'd just failed in my life's mission. "Well, tell her to get herself a writer and start! She's one of the Funny Ladies!"

Jane's own take on her performance that afternoon was a little less hyperbolic. "I thought you'd find me amusing," she said, "but I didn't think I'd have to hold for laughs." She appreciated Stuart's comments, but wasn't sure she was quite ready to set her sights on nightly gigs at Caroline's.

Despite this triumph, Jane knew the lay of the land and had no illusions about actually being cast as Snooks. We were both convinced, however, that she'd just indisputably nailed the right to understudy the role. Her competitor from the Carnegie team, Sue Henry, was having some serious dental problems that had forced her to beg off from the auditions.

"The poor thing," cooed Jane after hearing of Sue's predicament. "I should send her some caramels."

Marc had been obsessing over his own audition for weeks. Although his hair had begun to thin, he knew he still had the kind of apple-cheeked baby face that would allow him to convincingly play the teenage Stinky on stage. This kind of weird and silly character was tailor-made for his talents. John and Ricka had both loved his work in *My Great Dead Sister*, and he was, after all, the playwright's best friend. Not to mention that the second page of the *Moose Murders* manuscript stated in no uncertain terms, "For Marc Castle."

The pressure was slowly doing him in.

On the morning of his audition, he lay in bed for hours in a state of near catatonia. He arrived at the studio half an hour early and stood outside the building to chain-smoke three cigarettes (in case they weren't allowed inside). He'd made himself a solemn promise to quit the habit whatever the outcome of this ordeal, so he figured he might as well live it up now. He rode the elevators upstairs and sat down in the waiting room with a good fifteen minutes to spare. The air conditioning wasn't working, and he soon became aware that the "instant hair texture" he'd carefully applied to his scalp just before leaving his apartment was slowly dissolving into a moist, sticky mess.

"Marc Castle?" asked Amy, at the exact moment he'd begun to calculate the time it would take to do a little damage control in the men's room. "We're ready for you!"

Stuart (the only one besides Amy meeting Marc for the first time today) dutifully introduced him to each of us, and we all played along.

"Great play," Marc muttered after shaking my hand.

"What?" asked Stuart, as if he'd just heard an obscenity.

"Great play," repeated Marc, as Amy showed Stuart a copy of the play's dedication page.

"Oh!" said Stuart. "So *you're* the famous Marc Castle!"

Having now been given this grand introduction, it was time for the famous Marc Castle to dance for Grandma.

He started off well, getting a good laugh or two, but became increasingly flustered as his nerves took over. He forgot some of his bits (I knew this because we'd gone over all of them at his apartment days before). Mary McTigue seemed to have other things on her mind this afternoon, and her slow cue pickup screwed up Marc's timing as well. He ended by giving her a big, lingering, idolatrous squeeze that got him another laugh, and compensated somewhat for the long stretches of silence in between.

I knew he hadn't come anywhere near showing us his best work. But John and Ricka spent many minutes after he left the room commenting on his excellence in *My Great Dead Sister*. It was obvious they were both interested in him, and, so far, no other reading for Stinky had knocked anybody's socks off.

I told him all this after the auditions, when I ran into him standing with his bike two blocks away from the studio. He was very distraught.

"I know I blew it," he said. "I was so nervous I was physically ill. I should have had a beer beforehand. I've *never* been so nervous."

"Listen," I said, "round one is over. You just needed to get this first step out of the way."

"They *hated* me."

"They didn't hate you. They already know how good you are—you should have heard them going on about you. They're such fans it's sickening."

"So I'm getting a callback, right?"

"You know you are. And next time you'll be able to concentrate on the performance instead of the *event*."

The next audition wasn't scheduled until the following Tuesday, which gave John time to fly to L.A. to hear Eve Arden read for the role of Hedda. By this time I'd become anesthetized to the effects of Hollywood chatter, so Stuart's coup of setting up this meeting didn't make that big of an impression on me. I was much more excited about a subsequent meeting John was scheduled to take with Dennis at Sardi's on Tuesday morning before the auditions, the purpose of which was to once and for all smooth out all the rough edges of my production contract. To this day I still couldn't tell you exactly what those rough edges might have been, but I assume they all had to do with making sure I would be receiving an ample portion of the spoils of Moose. My main interest was in relieving Dennis of his duties as my agent and securing his position as Nelson's understudy before John beat me to the punch by hiring Brad O'Hare.

Dennis called me from the restaurant late Tuesday morning to tell me that he and John had reached a mutually satisfactory resolution and that my contract was now good to go.

"So," I said to John when I saw him an hour later at the studio, "I guess I'm now legally yours."

"Yes," said John dryly, "and Dennis sleeps with the fishes."

A little later, when I reached over to help myself to one of his breath mints, John cut me off short by slapping my hand. "I don't know about this," he said. "I didn't speak to Dennis about it."

Apparently the dust was still settling from this morning's negotiations. I decided to wait until the hiatus between auditions and callbacks before making my next move in sculpting Dennis's career.

These last few days of auditions could have provided fodder for a fairly decent "where-are-they-now?" documentary. Tall and skinny Carleton Carpenter, wearing a bow tie and saddle shoes, brought just the right balance of pathos and affability to the character of Howie Keene. Although he'd listed the 1950 film *Two Weeks with Love* on his resume, Marc had to clue me in later that this was where he'd sung "The Aba Daba Honeymoon" as a duet with Debbie Reynolds, a number I'd seen dozens of times thanks to its inclusion in *That's Entertainment* (the collection of highlights from the golden age of MGM musicals). Grayson Hall, whom I had watched religiously as the beleaguered Dr. Julia Hoffman on TV's supernatural soap *Dark Shadows* in the 60s, broke all semblance of formality by leaning over to squeeze my cheeks and exclaiming "You, I love!" She elaborated on this a bit by admitting "I'm afraid this is one of those plays that you either love or hate. As for me . . . well, here I am!" Roz Kelly, a.k.a. Pinky Tuscadero, Arthur "Fonzie" Fonzarelli's girlfriend on ABC's *Happy Days*, impressed us more with the mock deco graphics of her resume than she did with her acting ability, and Sylvia Miles of *Midnight Cowboy* fame ("You were gonna ask *me* for money?") waddled in like a bag lady (complete with several bags) and asked "Mind if I wear glasses?" before removing her psychedelic aviator goggles to reveal a Russian nesting doll collection of progressively smaller eyewear. The only note that John jotted down after this visit was "Forbidden Planet."

John's meeting with Eve had gone very well, and Stuart reported that he'd heard back from her manager Glenn and her husband Brooks, both of whom were pushing her to take the job. In the meantime, we continued to see a wide variety of alternative Heddas, including the lithe and looming Anne Francine, who'd replaced Bea Arthur as Vera Charles in the mid-60s Broadway production of *Mame*. Anne's NBC sitcom *Harper Valley PTA* had just been cancelled, and she was eager to "return to her roots" on the New York stage.

"It was crap," she told us, referring to the sitcom, "but it was eighteen-thousand-dollars-a-week crap."

She asked a lot of questions about her character, and wondered if we really thought she could pull off the "sex kitten" transformation in the second act. "Sure! You bet! Go for it!" we cheered. Anne then clasped Mary McTigue's hands and in great, stentorian tones exclaimed "We who are about to die salute you!"

Helen Gallagher, who'd worked with Anne Francine in *Mame* and had made a splash a few years later in *No, No, Nanette*, schlepped in as if she'd just been directed to take her place in line at the DMV. If I'd been asked to draw her as a comic strip character, I'd have made her eyes pencil dots, used a short, horizontal line for her mouth, and thrown in a dialogue balloon filled with dark little scribbles floating over her head.

"I swear," whispered Ricka, leaning into me. "I feel like giving a class on how to walk into auditions."

On the final day, we were moved to a higher floor of the building. The only thing different about the new room was its wall-to-wall carpeting, a feature that totally thwarted the two little tap dancers who hadn't been

able to join us for next week's Little Gay marathon. Conversely, it proved
to be quite an inspiration for the last Hedda we'd be seeing, playwright
Arthur Miller's baby sister, Joan Copeland.

I'd seen Joan play the wife of Danny Kaye's Noah in the 1970 musical
Two by Two, as well as the "bewitched, bothered, and bewildered" socialite
Vera Simpson in the 1976 Broadway revival of *Pal Joey*. Both times I'd been
taken by her elegance and quiet sophistication. Before Amy ushered her
into the room that last afternoon, Stuart extolled the many virtues of Miss
Copeland, advising us that she had become a confirmed recluse over the
past few years, and that she rarely bothered to come in for auditions unless
something had *particularly* incited her interest. Duly impressed by Stuart's
perfect impersonation of Erich von Stroheim, we all breathlessly awaited
the entrance of our own Norma Desmond.

Joan had chosen the "sex kitten" (as Anne Francine had called it) trans-
formational scene at the end of the play where Hedda and her son-in-law,
Nelson, reveal their hidden lust for each other. When Mary McTigue was
introduced as her scene partner, Joan was aghast.

"A woman?" she cried. "Oh, no, I can't do this with a woman! You *are*
a woman, aren't you, dear?"

As Mary dramatically left the room to take one of her five-minute
breaks that were becoming more frequent by the hour, Stuart bravely volunteered to act as her substitute. "Is she in tears?" asked Joan. "Did she just
lose her job because of me?"

"It's a cruel business," said John.

Nothing could have prepared any of us for the unchained lunacy that
followed. Apparently determined to dispel any notion that she was too
highbrow to indulge in farce, Miss Copeland tore into Stuart as if he were a
fresh slab of beef just tossed into her lair. She caressed him, she stroked him,
she ran her fingers through his hair, and then, like Cyd Charisse, entangled
her leg around his, grabbed hold of a chunk of his ass with one hand and
gave him a good, long, exploratory grope in the crotch with the other—all
the while undulating to a primal rhythm nobody else was privy to.

In a matter of seconds, Stuart's face went from pale pink to fire engine red.

As a parting gesture, Joan took full advantage of the plush carpeting
by dropping to her knees and burying her face deep into Stuart's groin,
growling and tugging at his trousers like a young dog with a chew toy.

I don't think anybody heard a word of Joan's dialogue. The roar of our laughter was so loud, in fact, that Mary cut her break short and came running back in to see what the hell was going on.

"I want to sincerely thank all of you for this special opportunity," said Joan once we'd all quieted down. "You know where to reach me."

We had to wait for Stuart to compose himself before letting in any of the few remaining actors. He'd withdrawn to the side of the room and was fanning himself with his script. "She grabbed my crotch," he kept saying over and over. "She grabbed my crotch...with her teeth!"

"You need a cigarette?" asked John.

Nothing—and no *one*—came anywhere close to matching the intensity of Joan Copeland's audition the rest of that last afternoon at the Bennett Studio. We saw Fisher Stevens and Brian Backer (two authentically teenage Stinky contenders), and a few more Dagmars—including Holland Taylor, who gave a great reading but struck me as being more of an edgy June Cleaver than Nurse Dagmar.

Stuart was called out of the room at the end of the day, and came back a few minutes later obviously trying to hide his glee. In true businesslike fashion, he asked John to join him outside for a minute.

After another few minutes they came back in, and John walked over to the table with his head lowered.

We'd had enough of the histrionics by then, Ricka and I.

"What?! Just say it!"

John shrugged and said, "We've signed Eve Arden."

After a little victory dance, Ricka walked over to Stuart and solemnly put her arm around his shoulder.

"Well, Stud," she said, "We're gonna let *you* break the news to Miss Copeland."

Chapter Four:

Casting Off

Somewhere in the bundle of mug shots we carried with us into Sardi's restaurant that late October afternoon lurked the remaining cast members of *Moose Murders*—all we had to do now was to flush them out in time for the callback auditions beginning the following week. Sardi's, the most popular watering hole for show people, was the best place to chow down if you wanted to flaunt your involvement in any current project of *note*. The food here was irrelevant; you went to steep yourself in tradition, feast your eyes on hundreds of celebrity caricatures hanging from the walls, and—most important—to stuff your ego. Every time you strolled into the place, there was at least a ninety percent chance that you'd be noticed by the Broadway Brass.

The brass was a little tarnished that afternoon. The only "celebrity" to show up was Leo Shull, the bombastic blowhard who owned and published *Show Business*, a weekly trade tabloid notorious for ripping off casting notices from its far worthier successor *Back Stage*. I had firsthand knowledge of Leo's distorted sense of ethics because I'd been one of his miserably paid editorial thieves several years before. During that time I'd never once witnessed him living up to his early reputation as the "actors' crusader," but I could vouch for the fact he fought damn hard to make sure his rag carried more "news" than his competition—no matter what the cost to his own dark and wizened soul.

And now, here he was again, pushing his way through the crowd, sporting a nearly-floor-length beaver coat and slobbering on a Cuban cigar he'd probably gotten from his best friend and fellow septuagenarian, Henny Youngman. While he was tossing his pelts over one of the chairs at a nearby table, he glanced in my direction for a split second, and I spastically turned my entire body in the opposite direction.

Here I was, sitting at Sardi's with the producer and associate producer of my first Broadway play, and yet suddenly I was overcome with nausea and reliving those awful days of not-so-long ago when I'd plagiarized casting items to pay my rent. Both John and Ricka were naturally compelled to ask what my problem was, so I told them my sob story without sparing a single Dickensian detail.

"What an asshole," reflected Ricka, just as a bottle of champagne was delivered, compliments of her husband Albert. "Don't worry. We have a *much* better table."

By the time we'd covered this better table with glossy photos of all the actors we were considering for callbacks ("not the most discreet method," John admitted), it wasn't just the Dom Perignon that was going to my head. Sardi's was working its magic on me, and I stopped worrying about any impending visit from Leo Shull. As we mixed and matched head shots like Olympian Gods toying with the mortals below, I found myself making broad, sweeping gestures and pontificating on the fine art of casting, as if somebody was behind me filming a documentary on my steady rise from newspaper galley slave to emerging Broadway playwright. When Leo actually did brush by our table on his way out, I was actually a little surprised he didn't stop to pay his "respects."

Approximately forty names ended up on the callback list we later delivered to Stuart and Amy. Encouraged by this accomplishment, and by the news from our general manager, Eddie Davis, that the official opening date for *Moose Murders* had been set for February 7 (with a week of previews beginning January 28), we decided to wander over to both the Booth and Plymouth theaters, two of the potential houses for our production. Eddie had assured us that other theaters could very well become available after the holidays.

"Looks like the O'Neill may be up for grabs soon," said John as we continued to shop for real estate in the theater district.

"So *The Wake of Jamie Foster* is a self-prophesy," suggested Ricka, referring to the Beth Henley play that had recently opened at the Eugene O'Neill.

"The reviews are killing it," said John. "I spoke to Norman this morning, and he said he was passing by here yesterday and saw Beth standing on the curb, crying her eyes out. He stuck around and eavesdropped while one of her SMU chums tried to console her. 'Beth,' the friend says, 'what's wrong?' 'Last year I couldn't lose,' she says. '*Crimes of the Heart* made me

Queen of the Prom. Now they're throwing mud on my dress and tearing out my hair!'"

"'But Beth,'" the friend says, 'remember when we were all together in school and we said the only thing that mattered was the opportunity to one day do what we do best—screw the rest! Do you remember that?'"

"'Yes,' she says. 'But I lied!'"

This little cautionary tale pulled me right back down to earth. As exciting as it was right now to anticipate the arrival of empty theaters, it was terrifying to hear about how they actually got that way.

The area around 44th Street between Sixth and Seventh Avenues where the Belasco Theater was located was under heavy construction that first day of callbacks, which made the grand old building built in 1907 look like Boris Aronson's set for the musical *Follies*. All the scaffolding, beams, and girders made it impossible for me to figure out how to get inside, although I was vaguely aware I should be looking for something marked "Stage Door." Two scruffy men were sharing a smoke in the alley, and, thinking they might be a couple of Joe Buffalo Dances who'd come dressed for the part, I considered waiting around with them for a while. Neither of them seemed too eager to fraternize with me, so I called the Pulvino & Howard office to obtain the backstage number of the theater. A few minutes later Amy appeared from some dark recess, and, after rolling her eyes just a little bit, took me by the hand to lead me into the theater.

This was my first time inside David Belasco's palace, and, although it had obviously fallen into ill repair over the past several years, its spoiled splendor still managed to weaken my knees. The dark, rich, paneled woodworking on the walls was glowing warmly from the light cast by dozens of Tiffany lamps, and everywhere I turned I discovered another lavish mural—eighteen in all, I later learned, each done by an artist named Everett Shin. I remembered from my college theater history class that everything I was looking at had been designed to Belasco's specifications. Educated in a monastery as a child, and prone to wearing faux clerical garb as an adult, the trailblazing impresario had come to be known as "the Bishop of Broadway," and indeed, standing there in his magnificent neo-Georgian cathedral, I felt more spiritual than I had in years.

Catching me in this reverie, Stuart approached with his head bowed, and his hands clasped like a monk. "You know," he said, "Belasco's old business office and private apartment take up the top floor."

"Can we take the tour?" I asked.

"Nope. Closed off. Besides," he said, dropping his voice a bit, "you wouldn't want to."

"Why?"

"A lot of eyewitnesses claim Belasco's ghost still haunts the place. And there are some very unsettling stories about what he was like when he was alive . . ."

Before Stuart could elaborate, Lillie called hello to us from the first row of orchestra seats. I was a little surprised to see her here, until it dawned on me that she'd probably been called in to help John determine the most credible Holloway family portrait.

"Can you *believe* that bone structure?" whispered Stuart.

I sat down next to Lillie just as Amy welcomed our first contender, an Erma Bombeck look-alike named Wendy Wolfe who had the kind of indiscreet charm of the upstate New York bourgeoisie I was looking for to play Snooks.

Something had happened to Wendy since we'd last seen her. All the piss and vinegar had evaporated, and she'd turned into a real lady—more Emily Post than Erma Bombeck.

"I haven't auditioned for anything in over a year," she said, after John suggested that she try to show us a little more of the brazen quality of her first audition. "I'd forgotten how horrible, how demeaning, how devastating this experience is. I'm *petrified*."

She opened up a little when belting out a few bars of both "Jeepers Creepers" and "People," but she never did manage to regain the confidence that had impressed us all at the Bennett Studio.

"I see this all the time, especially at callbacks," Stuart said after Wendy had made a tearfully apologetic exit. "It's the old 'the less I do, the less they won't like' syndrome."

Holland Taylor walked on stage next.

"What did you people *do* to that woman?" she demanded. "I think she may need a tranquilizer."

"She hates auditioning," explained John.

"Well, I'm with her on that," laughed Holland. "Do you know how hard it was for me to leave my nice, safe, comfortable rehearsal to come here and put myself on the line?"

The rehearsal Holland was referring to was for the Lee Kalcheim comedy *Breakfast with Les and Bess* that would be opening in December at the Hudson Guild Theatre in the Chelsea area downtown. This show had a limited run, so Holland would presumably be able to work things out logistically should she be cast in *Moose Murders*. For now, at least, this didn't seem to be where the cards were falling. Holland commanded the stage with her elegantly aggressive interpretation of the supporting role of Nurse Dagmar, but by doing so, clearly demonstrated that she was far better suited to play the leading role of Hedda.

And that little apple had already fallen to Eve.

Jean DeBaer, who followed Holland, was a much more feasible Dagmar. She was authoritative, svelte, and faintly exotic.

She also had a nice rack—which, let's face it, told you just about all you needed to know about Nurse Dagmar.

She made her way on stage like one of Minsky's headliners, and confronted her polar opposite, Mary McTigue.

"Who are you?" Jean asked innocently.

Mary folded her arms across her chest and gave Jean a long, icy stare.

"I'm *reading* with you," she finally snarled.

Mary continued to be short and testy throughout Jean's audition. She'd been out of sorts all morning, and her broadly telegraphed indignation was starting to really bug me. I asked Stuart if there was some specific problem she wasn't willing or able to talk to us about.

"Oh, no," he said. "I think she just needs a good cup of coffee."

The next actor to test his luck with Mary was Scott Evans, who was about the same age as Marc and who, also like Marc, had the kind of youthful quality that allowed him to get away with playing a teenager on stage. He took his time with his entrance, inching his way toward Mary like Norman Bates working up the nerve to ask Marion Crane to come on up to the house to check out his stuffed bird collection. He milked his fidgety and psychotic tics and spasms for all they were worth, and had us chuckling long before he even opened his mouth.

These antics raised his stock with me personally. Before then I'd merely thought of him as having an interesting voice. Still, I remained solidly predisposed not to favor him or any other Stinky over Marc.

Scott had done his homework. He epitomized the rich, cloistered kid gone bad, and, little by little, meticulously exposed different facets of Stinky that far transcended drugs, sex, and rock 'n' roll—although these elements were all nicely represented in his performance as well.

"He's not just relying on external humor," commented Lillie. "He's making your lines funny, too."

"Gee, thanks," I said, crossing my eyes for emphasis.

"Oh, you know what I mean," she said.

Unfortunately, I did know what she meant, and it was making me very nervous. Scott was now presenting a challenge for Marc (who was waiting in the wings with a couple other Stinkys), and—considering the way he'd let his nerves get the better of him the last time—I wasn't sure he was going to be up for it. I'd spoken to Marc that morning before leaving for the theater, and he'd seemed fine, very determined—in much better shape than he'd been two weeks ago.

Even as I watched an actor by the name of Michael Linden Green give his impression of one, long, post-nasal drip, and another fellow named Christopher Brenner play Stinky as a precocious five-year-old, my stomach continued to churn. Marc *had* to do better than these guys.

While I was sweating it out in front, Stuart was backstage approaching a young man with a striking full head of long and thick sandy hair, most of which had been gathered in the back and secured with a couple of rubber bands. Several locks were swept in a seemingly deliberate fashion across the left side of his face, prompting Stuart to ask if he was hiding a scar.

"This is a wig," beamed Marc.

"Oh my God!" gasped Stuart. "Marc Castle? Is that *you* in there?"

This clinched the deal for Marc, who had been having last-minute doubts about the efficacy of his camouflage. If he'd been able to fool Stuart, who was standing only a foot away, he should be home free with those of us sitting in the orchestra.

And sure enough, like an unshorn Samson set loose on the Pharisees, Marc flexed his comedy muscles and devastated us all with a cavalcade of sight gags and outrageous bits of stage business—most of which (like the wig) he'd managed to keep a secret. At one point, while giving Mary a crushing bear hug, he turned his head toward us and shivered with delight, smiling from ear to ear like a Cheshire cat.

"Look at that baby face!" screamed Ricka.

He told me later he'd felt like he'd been giving a recital at the "Frances Bavier School of Mugging. Except I had more hair than Aunt Bea."

Marc was clearly the sensation of the day, and John worked with him longer than he had with any of the other actors—including Scott Evans. I truly think that if Scott hadn't shown up that day, Marc would have been signed on the spot. But Scott *had* shown up, and both he and Marc—the last two remaining Stinky aspirants—were scheduled to duel it out the following (and final) day of auditions.

As soon as I stepped foot inside the theater the next morning, a pale and wraithlike figure sprang at me from the shadows. My assailant turned out not to be the ghost of David Belasco, but rather the broken and earthbound spirit of Reader McTigue, who was obviously very near the end of her own mortal coil. Her jaws were clenched, and her eyes were wild with determination—I don't think I would have been any less comfortable encountering the old "Bishop" himself.

"Can I speak with you for a minute—in *private*?" she hissed.

"Sure," I said, and followed her back into the shadows. When she was sure nobody else could see or hear us, she popped the question that I guessed had been on her mind from the first day of auditions.

"Would you consider reading me for Dagmar?"

To be fair to Mary, being an audition reader is one of the most thankless jobs the business has to offer. You're asked to exhibit just enough skill not to throw off any of the dozens of actors you're reading with, all the while remaining virtually invisible yourself. Good work for a ghost, maybe, or for an accounting temp looking for a break from sharpening pencils and running for coffee, but not so good for an aspiring actor.

"Let's see if we can take care of this right now," I said, relieved to have finally gotten to the bottom of Mary's chronic bad mood, and happy to do whatever I could to make it go away for this last day of auditions. I talked to John, who, equally interested in keeping the peace, invited her up on stage immediately.

She didn't require her own reader, because she'd reworked the designated "Dagmar" scenes into a single monologue. She knew just about every line in the play by heart, so nobody was surprised that she was off book. No longer encumbered by the script, she was now free to be just as demonstrative with her right arm as she had been all along with her left. She was also decidedly louder. Other than that, her solo performance as Dagmar was the spitting image of the hundred or so previous readings she'd given over the past month.

"Thank you," said John, when she had finished. "It was almost as if you've done this part before."

"Do you have any notes?" she asked. "Anything different you'd like me to try?"

"No," said John. "I think we're good."

She remained standing center stage, apparently waiting for John to rethink this response.

"Thanks again," cued Ricka, and Mary finally made her exit into the wings.

Just a moment or two later she was back.

"Excuse me," she said. "Lisa McMillan is here, but I need to settle something before you see her."

"What's up?" John asked.

"I was just talking to Amy, and I'm afraid I'm going to have to ask that she not bite me."

"Amy wants to *bite* you?" I asked, wondering why I hadn't thought of that.

"No," said Mary. "*Lisa* bit Amy. Last night."

"Lisa couldn't make the auditions yesterday, so I read her at home," explained John, doing his best to stifle a laugh. "Mary wasn't there so Amy played Nelson. And Lisa is very…resourceful, so, at one point she, you know, *bit* Amy. On the arm."

To his credit, he was able to get out this entire explanation before cracking up with the rest of us.

"It left a mark!" verified Amy, who'd followed Mary on stage.

"This is where I'm going to have to draw the line," Mary declared, staunchly ignoring the loud snickering erupting from the orchestra seats below. We had become a group of obnoxious school kids ganging up on the substitute teacher.

"I must insist that Lisa not bite me," said Mary, without a trace of irony. "I have a show to do this evening."

"I'm sorry," I whispered to Lillie, who had joined us again today. "Miss McTigue can't go on this evening. Rabid, you know."

"Maybe somebody else could do the honors—just this once," suggested Mary.

"Don't look at me," said Stuart. "I'm still getting over Joan Copeland."

"No sweat," said Amy. "I'll do it. Let her give me her best shot!"

While Mary enthusiastically took one of her final five-minute breaks, the six-foot tall Lisa McMillan came on stage to stand beside the five-foot tall Amy Schecter. They were a cartoon couple: tall and short, skinny and wide—Natasha and Boris chasing after "Moose and Squirrel"—only without "Squirrel."

Lisa wore Dagmar's requisite black evening gown, a pair of gigantic white sneakers, and a visor to suggest a nurse's cap.

"You again, Shorty?" she asked, while resting her arm on top of Amy's head.

These preliminary visuals were so hysterically funny, it was almost unnecessary for Lisa to do her scene. She didn't bite Amy this time around, but did just about everything else she thought she could get away with. Her arms and legs, like strands of toothpaste freshly squeezed from individual tubes, oozed their way under, around, and over just about every one of Amy's moving parts.

Just at the point when Nurse Dagmar (fantasizing about the systematic deaths of each member of the Holloway clan) reaches more than a metaphorical climax, Lisa turned full front, and, in a voice that must have emanated from somewhere in the bowels of the Belasco, bellowed the single word "Ow."

"Ow?" asked John. "That's an interesting choice."

"I have just been bitten," said Lisa, still in character. "On one of my McNuggets."

"Oh, boo *hoo*," said Amy, popping her head out from under the tangled coils of Lisa's appendages. "You can dish it out, but you can't take it!"

"I don't know," said John once the commotion had died down. "Lisa's great, but if we cast her as Dagmar we're going to have to let Amy play Nelson. I don't think we should break up their act."

June Gable's agent had phoned the theater that morning to advise us that his client had been called back a number of times as a potential replacement for one of the cast members in the musical *Nine*—a job that would carry with it a guaranteed one-year contract. This warning had its desired effect on me, at least, especially since it followed Wendy Wolfe's nose dive the day before.

I told Stuart I was afraid we'd seen the last of June; he wasn't at all concerned. "Her agent's just testing the water," he said. "It's the oldest ploy in the book."

Sure enough, June strutted on stage later that morning, still clad in her skintight chinos and leopard top. "My teacher at Carnegie Mellon always said you should wear the same outfit to callbacks," she explained—which, of course, incited a mini college reunion among the various Carnegie alumni present in the auditorium.

In the middle of her scene, she broke character to set up one of her planned bits of business.

"I think Snooks's only source of reference for being a detective would be *Columbo*," she said. Like the typical impressionist, she turned her back a moment to "get into character," and then finished the interrogation scene as Peter Falk—complete with the one-eye squint that must have been very difficult to maintain for such a long stretch.

"How did you write Snooks?" she asked me, while John and Ricka were discussing what they'd like to see from her next. "Admit it—you *are* Snooks!"

"I'm pretty lousy at impressions, though," I said.

"There's so much room with this part," she went on. "You can be happy, sad, funny—plus sick. A *lot* sick. I figure Snooks sits in her motel room eating chocolates and working on her routines."

I was about to challenge this notion that the caustically spontaneous Snooks would ever have the patience to actually sit around *working* on a routine, when John called June back on stage to be paired with Don Potter—one of our two favored candidates for the role of Howie. Don was short, sprightly, and utterly adorable—so it had come as no surprise that he'd originated the title role in the world premiere of the musical *Snoopy!!!* at the Off-Broadway Lamb's Theatre the year before. Lovable and nurturing, he was the perfect foil for the fierce and feisty Snooks. Together, Don and June looked like grown-up versions of Cubby and Karen, the littlest Mouseketeers from the original *Mickey Mouse Club*.

Right after Don left, June was teamed up with the lanky Carleton Carpenter, whose prissy mannerisms and impeccable timing had swept me off my feet at the Bennett Studio. I loved the way this man came off on stage, and if June hadn't unofficially become the show's linchpin, he would have been my hands-down choice for Howie. Try as I might, though, I just couldn't picture him as June's husband. It crossed my mind that he would make a very intriguing Nelson, but that would mean having Eve play Hedda as a woman closer to her actual age, which—aside from screwing up the casting for all the Holloway children—would undoubtedly be a deal breaker for Miss Arden. So I kept my mouth shut, and resigned myself to the fact that Carleton and I would have to forego our own "Aba Daba Honeymoon."

"You ready to do this?" asked John, once June was left standing alone on stage. With the Sword of *Nine* looming over our heads, we all thought it best to act quickly, so unanimously voiced our consent.

After taking June aside for only a minute or two, John came back smiling. "She'll do it," he said.

"Wait a minute!" cautioned Ricka, as the rest of us were exchanging hugs and back slaps. "Eddie needs to call her agent *now*! I'll phone him!"

Ricka was gloating when she joined us a few minutes later.

"June's still here, making phone calls," she reported. "I overheard her telling somebody 'I got it! I told you I would! This'll bring back my name!'"

"So much for any objections from the agent," said Stuart.

"Oh, spare me!" said Lillie. "This is a chance to *originate* a role. Of course she's taking it!"

We were just beginning to come down from this high, having all but ignored the handful of Joes and Dagmars that had shown up after June finally left, when Dennis quietly walked down the stage ramp to join us in the orchestra.

"Well," he said, "I did it."

"Really?" asked John. "Did you leave any witnesses?"

"About three of them," said Dennis. "Two of them were in tears."

"What *are* you talking about?" asked Lillie.

"I just officially quit my day job," he explained. "God, I've always wanted to say that. You're looking at a free man—in another two weeks, anyway."

"Congratulations!" Lillie said to Dennis, before turning her attention back to me. "So," she said, "when are *you* leaving Air France? We have a play to put on, you know."

"Soon," I promised, fighting back acidic pangs of jealousy. I knew Lillie would never have to worry about anything as mundane as "egg money." But because my own financial cushion was nil, and since it would be some time before any royalties from the show started to come my way, I couldn't afford to bite off the hand that had been feeding me for the past few years until I'd secured a *Moose Murders* weekly salary for Dennis. I was all too aware that if I didn't close this understudy deal with John soon, I might very well find myself booking yet another medical convention to Bombay via Paris on the night my show opened on Broadway.

These gruesome thoughts were set aside as I watched Jack Dabdoub—a burly teddy bear of a man and the veteran of thirteen Broadway shows—take the stage as our best Joe Buffalo Dance to date. He was naturally funny and seemingly strong enough to carry out the many extracurricular activities assigned to this role (including running around in the second act, brandishing an axe and wearing a moose head), and would fit in nicely with the assortment of loonies we were slowly bringing into the fold.

By this time, Marc was once again waiting in the wings, showing off his lustrous new golden locks to a cluster of similarly coifed little girls, the crème de la crème of our previous search for the youngest member of the Holloway brood. Scott Evans was there too, but with his mousy brown and relatively short-cropped hair, the poor boy was obviously destined to win merely the title of "Mr. Congeniality" in today's pageant.

Most of the little girls had brought tape cassettes with them, to accompany their jazz and tap routines. One of them even brought along batons and hula hoops. None of these young ladies, however, could hold a candle to Mara Hobel, whose angelic face belied the sailor's mouth and swagger she could assume on cue. It was impossible for me not to think about the amazing scene in *Mommie Dearest* where Faye Dunaway as Joan Crawford—enraged by a speck of dirt she's discovered in the bathroom—goes into a rampage and covers everything in sight with Bon Ami cleansing powder—including her daughter Christina, played by Mara. The camera zooms in for a close-up of Mara as she sits forlornly on the floor and utters an incredulous "Jesus Christ." Only ten years old, and already carrying the weight of Joan Crawford's world (along with about a pound of Bon Ami) on her tiny little shoulders.

Well, by God, in this show, we'd let *her* be the monster.

Marc and Mara made a delightfully abhorrent pair of siblings as they fought over the attentions of their mother, as read by the suitably inattentive Mary McTigue. In this scene, Stinky, stoned out of his mind, has to explain the rules to "Murder in the Dark," a parlor game played with all the lights off, which requires a randomly chosen "murderer" to stalk and then "kill" a victim of his or her choice with a couple of quick squeezes on the arm. Always looking for new ways to manhandle his mother, Stinky uses Hedda as his demonstration model, and, predictably, gets carried away with the arm squeezes. Marc played all of this to perfection, with the same pizzazz he'd shown the day before. Even Dennis, who'd once claimed that Marc would get into the show "over my dead body," crossed over from the dark side of familial rivalry to become just another out-of-control Marc Castle groupie.

Marc had found plenty of time backstage to size up the competition, and decided he wouldn't stick around to watch Scott's final moment of truth. Just as he (Marc) was stepping into the alley through the stage door, Scott—in the middle of his own "Murder in the Dark" scene—opted to spare his mother and to "murder" his obnoxious little sister Gay instead. This took everyone by surprise—including poor little Mara—and the result was volcanic.

Marc heard the screams of laughter from the alleyway, and his heart sank. "I knew I'd just lost the role," he confessed to me later.

We stayed in the Belasco after the auditions, to make our final decisions. John asked us all to give our choices along with the reasons behind those choices, and Stuart volunteered to go first: Don Potter for Howie (who could believe Carleton?); Mara for Gay (in addition to the fact that she was very talented, the press would never hurt); Jack Dabdoub for Joe (no question); and Scott Evans for Stinky.

"I loved Marc's first audition," Stuart said. "But the more I saw of him and Scott back to back, the more I realized there was a firmer foundation of reality in Scott's performance."

"Dagmar's the stickler for me," he continued. "It's between Jean De-Baer and Lisa McMillan. I've worked with Lisa, and know she's inventive—but she just doesn't have Jean's experience. I'd go with Jean."

John and Ricka's choices matched, with the exception of Dagmar. Neither was sure we'd even *seen* the killer Dagmar yet.

I'm sure the others expected a fight from me about Scott, but they didn't get one. Scott's amazing ability to pull stuff out of the air—bringing something entirely different to each reading—had absolutely floored me. Stuart's comment about a "firmer foundation of reality" also impressed me, in spite of the fact that we were dealing with stock characters in this lowest-of-the-low form of comedy. I agreed that Scott might just be able to make Stinky both funny *and* believable, which seemed a terrific concept at the time.

"But I think Marc should definitely understudy the role," I said, resolutely. Saying this didn't do much to relieve my guilt, but if John bought it, I would at least be able to leave with a bone to throw to Marc.

"There's a problem with that," said John. "I've talked to Eddie, and he thinks we should wait until the show is running before splurging on individual understudies for either Hedda or Stinky. We're better off now hiring somebody who could stand in for both Stinky *and* Howie—and maybe even Nelson, in a pinch."

Ready or not, I had my cue.

"You know we've talked about Dennis understudying Nelson," I said.

"He could do that," said John. "But, you know—we also need somebody to play Sidney."

"Aha! The 'fetid roll of gauze,'" said Dennis, who was, after all, standing right there in the same room. He was quoting Nurse Dagmar's profoundly succinct description of her body-bandaged charge, Sidney Holloway.

"He may be fetid, but he gets his name on the marquee," said John. "But it's up to you. You can play Sidney, or you can understudy Nelson *and* play Sidney, or you can just understudy Nelson—and we'll get somebody else to wear the gauze."

"Door number two! Door number two!" shouted Ricka.

"Hey," said Lillie. "You'll be immortalized as one of the original cast members! And bless their little old hearts, nobody *ever* remembers the understudies."

"You all know I'm claustrophobic," Dennis pointed out.

"You'll be wearing a bathrobe and slippers," said John. "We'll only have to cover your hands and head. And maybe your ankles, I don't know, we'll have to check with the costume designer."

"And I'm sure they'll cut out little holes for all *your* little holes," chuckled Ricka.

"You're all enjoying this, aren't you?" grumbled Dennis.

"Yes," we all said, none of us missing the beat.

"I don't know," Dennis said finally. "May I at least sleep on it?"

"Sure," said John. "But don't take too long." He smiled maliciously. "We need to wrap this thing up."

"This is pay-back time," said Dennis when we got home that evening. "He's never forgiven me for being your agent."

"Maybe not," I said. "But at least it's all on the table now."

I had planned to stop by Marc's apartment right after the auditions to deliver the news—whatever it was—in person, but the decision that Dennis now had to make had shifted my focus. And, under the circumstances, I didn't think our little quandary would have been of much interest to Marc. I called him instead, bracing myself for the worst.

"That's okay," said Marc while I was apologizing for calling with this news from the safety of my own home. "I figured when you and Dennis didn't show up that Scott had been cast. It would have been nice if you'd come over anyway," he added, not accusingly, but stating a simple fact.

"Listen," he said, "I figure if things work out the way they normally do in my life, Scott will come down with some strange, exotic disease just before opening and I'll end up doing Stinky yet."

"Yeah," I said. "Let's just keep looking at the *bright* side."

Dennis took the weekend to decide whether he wanted to show up backstage every night of the run of *Moose Murders* to play poker with the other understudies or to be rolled on stage every evening as the quadriplegic Holloway patriarch. A third option, of course, was to preserve his dignity and just bow out of the project altogether, and, trust me, he found this to be the most appealing solution by far. But having just quit his day job, he was in too deep to abandon the Moose now. On Sunday night he called John to tell him he had decided both to understudy Nelson and to make his Broadway debut as the mummified Holloway patriarch.

It was during this phone conversation that we learned that John and Ricka, after much deliberation, had decided to offer the role of Dagmar to Lisa McMillan, and that she'd accepted. We also learned that Carnegie alums Andy Matthews and Suzanne Henry (whose teeth were just fine now, thanks for asking) were both on board to join Dennis in those backstage poker games.

Unlike the rest of us, Jane had a few other pressing matters to attend to at the moment (not the least of which was going over the edited galleys of her book), so telling her that Sue Henry would be understudying Snooks was far easier than telling Marc he'd lost the role of Stinky. Still, it saddened me that I hadn't been able to book passage on the good ship *Moose Murders* for either one of them.

But at least Dennis was aboard, and now that our unsinkable vessel had a full passenger list, it looked as if we were ready to finally set sail into the icy waters ahead.

Chapter Five:

A Receiving Line

I certainly hadn't expected to lock antlers with Eve at our very first meeting. As Dennis and I drove north on the Pacific Coast Highway a few days after this battle of wills, those ominous words "we can take this all up again with John in New York" played back in my head like a loop from some God-awful B movie. Was Dennis right? Had I single-handedly managed to screw things up with the star even before rehearsals began? Was I just another temperamental hack? Were hacks even *allowed* temperaments? And what kind of reception would I have to face when I got back to the city in another week?

I managed to calm myself down a bit once we entered the state of Washington, the final stop on our itinerary. We spent these last few days at the Benedictine monastery on the campus of Saint Martin's College in Lacey, where we were guests of Dennis's old army buddy—a musical prodigy-turned-monk who now went by the name of Brother Aelred. Dennis had long considered Saint Martin's to be his "soul center," and even I—the designated nonspiritual member of our party of two—found the austere charm of this woodsy retreat extremely seductive. As I took in the sobering beauty of Mount Rainier looming on the horizon, or sat with the brothers in front of a crackling fire inside the abbey's community room, I was tempted to renounce my wicked, wicked ways, swallow my unearned pride, and just give in to all of Eve's ideas—provided, of course, I would ever get to see her again.

But this spell cast by Saint Martin's began to wear off as soon as we boarded our flight back to Manhattan. By the time I'd sorted through the clutter of mail and phone messages waiting for me at home—all of which were far more interesting now that at any other stage of my life—my humbling reverie had totally dissolved and I was ready to get right back to the show business at hand. I decided that reaching a reasonable compromise with Eve would be more viable than just turning belly-up and becoming one of those spineless yes-men she was obviously used to. Armed with this rediscovered conviction, I waited a fashionable twenty-four hours before marching into the Force Ten headquarters.

A lot had being going on while I was off frolicking with the Benedictines.

"Where do you want me to start?" said John, sitting behind his monolithic oak desk.

"Jump in anywhere," I said, filled with equal measures of excitement and dread.

"The theater," said Ricka, as she took her place behind her own monstrosity of a desk perpendicular to John's. I felt very vulnerable sitting on a chair inside this L-shaped fortress, and briefly considered asking them to drag in a third desk for *me*—just to even the playing field.

"We got the Eugene O'Neill after all," said John.

Although Beth Henley's *The Wake of Jamey Foster* had, as expected, closed on October 23 after twelve performances, we'd lost our bid for the O'Neill to the producers of *Monday After the Miracle*—William Gibson's sequel to *The Miracle Worker*. This show, John now informed me, had opened on December 14 and closed four days later after only seven performances. *Moose Murders* was next in line, and we all prayed that this was where the trend of steadily dwindling running days would end.

The O'Neill on 49th Street had once been owned by Neil Simon, and had housed many of his own plays, including *California Suite* and *Chapter Two*. It had a seating capacity of 1,300—which was a little larger than we'd anticipated, but, according to Eddie Davis, gave us a little more leeway in setting ticket prices.

"Home at last!" I cheered.

"You know John Getz passed as Nelson," John continued.

"John Getz?" I repeated. "What happened to Jeffrey Jones?"

"Oh, he reneged ages ago."

"Why?"

"Who knows?" shrugged John.

"He must tend his flowers," suggested Ricka.

"Not that it matters much now," I said, "but who is John Getz?"

"He's a good actor," said John. "But maybe not quite as good as *he* thinks he is. He wanted more money than June."

"So that leaves us with . . . ?"

"We've signed Nicholas Hormann," announced John. "He's in Gurney's *The Dining Room* at Playwrights Horizons right now, but he'll be free by the end of the month."

"And he's good?" I asked.

"He's a graduate of the Yale Drama School. How bad could he be?"

"And he's definitely doing the show—not just waiting for something better to turn up?"

"Like I said, he signed his contract. We're all set. We've also got a costume designer—my friend John Carver Sullivan—I think you'll like his work."

"Carnegie?"

"Yeah," John said, arching a brow. "You got a problem with that?"

"Hey, he's a graduate of Carnegie Mellon. How bad could he be?"

"Bite me," said John.

"Any other goodies?"

"Pat Collins is doing the lights, and Serino, Coyne, & Nappi will be handling advertising and PR."

"Don't forget this," said Ricka, reaching over her desk to hand me a cardboard mailing tube. Inside I found a rendering of the *Moose Murders* poster, which I carefully unrolled and studied as if it were the deed to a diamond mine.

Here are the details of this poster, in approximately the same order I took them in:

A goofy cartoon moose head was frowning at a number of bullet holes peppering the right side of the wooden plaque on which it was mounted. Underneath, "MOOSE MURDERS" was spelled out in big block letters— all of them blood red except for the second "R" in "Murders" which was lying on its side, drained of its ink—presumably as a result of being hit by a stray bullet lodged in its "leg." Eve's name was above the title and my own name (at half the font size) was directly below the title. Underneath my name, in the same font size but without the caps, was a separate line listing June and Nicholas. Below them, in alphabetical order in a still smaller font size, came six more members of the cast in groups of two. Finally, centered beneath these last folks, in the same letter size as June and Nicholas, came the following statement:

"and Lillie Robertson."

John, Ricka, and the designers took up the second half of the credit tableau, but I didn't get around to analyzing the politics of *their* placement because I just couldn't tear my eyes away from "and Lillie Robertson." I was fixated on this tribute.

"And Lillie Robertson?" "*And?*" "And Elizabeth Taylor" I would have understood. Or even "and Rula Lenska."

"Great billing," I finally said. "Your wife must have a crackerjack agent."

"I wanted to do something nice for Lillie," explained John.

It could have been worse, of course. He could have put her above the title with Eve or in a goddamn box. I decided I was overreacting, and tried to make light of the situation.

"Too bad she's not playing the moose," I said. "Then you could say "and Lillie Robertson as the moose."

Ricka, at least, laughed at that.

"Fuck you both," said John, with only half a smile.

"So when do rehearsals start?" I asked, as I rolled up the "deed" and slid it back inside its cardboard sheath.

"Monday, the third of January," Ricka answered. "We're switching over to the Minskoff because it's more conveniently located for Eve—she's staying at the Wyndham on 58th Street."

"She should be arriving there any minute," added John, checking his watch. "Oh. And speaking of Eve . . . "

Here it was.

"She called me after you guys met with her a couple weeks ago."

I was ready. I was Lloyd Richards about to face the wrath of Margo Channing.

"She'd like you to make some changes in her dialogue."

"Sure," I said, probably a little too quickly and enthusiastically to carry any credibility. "How many changes are we talking about?"

"Oh, not that many. Just, you know . . . act two."

"What—the whole act?"

"Not really. Mostly her lines—in *both* acts, actually. And maybe a few of Nelson's."

"And the ending," reminded Ricka.

"Oh, yeah–and the ending. She wants you to knock off Nelson."

"Uh huh," I said. "That's a thought, I guess."

"She doesn't think he has any redeeming qualities."

"Um . . . nobody in the play has any of *those*," I said. "I was real careful about that."

"Yeah, that's true—but she's convinced that if both she and Nelson get away with murder, audiences will despise *her*, by association. And, you know, I think she has a point. She is the star—I guess you can't blame her for wanting to be the last one standing."

"That's really all any of us can aspire to," noted Ricka.

"So that's about it," said John. "She said she went over most of this with you, so you should have a pretty good idea what she's looking for. A little less body talk, a little more dignity, that sort of thing."

"Less lewd, more prude," clarified Ricka.

"And what did you tell her?" I asked.

"I said I'd talk to you about it."

"Right. Well, now you have."

"Yeah."

While John and Ricka patiently waited, I made a mental tally of my options, only one of which seemed feasible at the moment. "Tell you what, "I said. "I'll go over the script, and see if I can make Hedda sound a little more like Eve Arden, how's that?"

"That would be good," said John. "Because—just between the three of us . . . "

"Yes?"

"This could be a deal breaker."

"Gotcha. Guess I'd better go hit the old Selectric," I said, as I rose from my chair. I stopped just short of the doorway.

"By the way," I said. "Is it 'Stinky' or 'Icky'?"

"I don't know what you're talking about," said John.

"Good," I said, as I took this small blessing with me out the door.

That afternoon I sat down at my desk with one of the *Moose Murders* scripts recently "published" by Studio Duplicating Services. There was something dangerously misleading about the attractive simulated leather binding of this professional-looking printing job which had my name and the title of my opus embossed in gold on its cover. This packaging proudly announced to the world that my work was *done*, and that whatever I'd find inside was now beyond either editing or reproach.

So I sat there for about an hour admiring the thing before finally willing myself to deface its contents with my red pencil. After the first few sprawling revisions, however, I began to get a far more objective picture of what I was up against.

"Let me ask you something," I said to Dennis at some point. "Does this play make any sense to you?"

"Not really," he freely admitted. "But that's never seemed to be a priority."

"Well, it's a *farce*."

"Sure is."

"It's supposed to be improbable."

"If you ask me, this whole thing is improbable. But what do I know? I'm just the understudy."

Whether or not Dennis had intended it as such, I found his assessment somewhat reassuring, and continued trying to introduce some "logic" into the pages of my jolly farce. I delivered my latest draft to Force Ten the next morning. It contained just about everything Eve had asked for, including Nelson's timely demise.

Now that Dennis was on the production payroll, it was time to tender my resignation from Air France. My departure came as no surprise to my fellow reservationists, many of whom—in between discounted weekend flights to Monaco and Malta—had been vicariously following each and every episode of my Broadway adventure from the beginning. It was a real Cinderella story for all of us. As members of the self-described "poor man's jet set," we'd all been sitting in our cubicles, taking one call after another and dreaming our own private dreams—and now here I was throwing off my headset and actually busting loose from the joint. The only thing missing was the arrival of Richard Gere in uniform to "lift me up where I belong," but I was a lot heavier than Debra Winger, so that probably wouldn't have worked out all that well anyway.

An article in that morning's *New York Daily News*—the first to announce the return of Eve Arden to Broadway—had been posted on a bulletin board in the cafeteria. The empty space around this lone item promised magical things to come. About twelve of my colleagues took me out to lunch, making certain not to take me back to work until I was totally shitfaced. Once I'd staggered into the lounge, I was presented with a leather briefcase and an ornately decorated moose figurine allegedly hand-crafted by an artist living in Argentina.

"That's very nice," said one of the few workers I didn't know very well. "But why a moose?"

"Peasant!" said my bitchy friend Maxine, who'd organized the ceremony.

There was also a double chocolate cake and a large card that had been signed by everybody in reservations. It read like a high school yearbook—a few entries even urged me to "stay as sweet as you are." And, sure enough, I stayed suitably sweet for at least the remainder of the afternoon, holding court and giving audience to the members of what I recognized even then to be the most devoted and guileless fan club I'd ever be able to call my own.

On Thursday, the 30th of December, John and Lillie hosted a lavish party at the Dakota to usher in the New Year and the New Show. Everybody involved in the production was invited—it was the first time we'd all be assembled in one place. I kept my cool right up to the point that Dennis and I stood outside the door to the apartment—at which time all hell broke loose and I had to suppress an overwhelming urge to turn back and run screaming into the night.

I had no idea what was prompting this sense of foreboding. Over the past several months, I'd been in this building at least a dozen times. John, Lillie, and Ricka had all long since become my trusted friends, and, with the possible exception of Miss Arden, there wasn't anybody out to get me on the guest list this evening. What in God's name was my problem?

It was the whole *Rosemary's Baby* thing. I'd never been able to shake off this association, and right now I wouldn't have been surprised to open the door to John's apartment to find a coven of elderly men and ladies playing flutes and chanting away in the nude.

"God is dead! The Moose lives!"

As it turned out, nobody was naked. People were dressed very nicely, in fact—no one more splendiferously than our hostess, the Lady Robertson. She'd done her hair up in a French twist and was absolutely radiant. She greeted us so warmly, and was so genuinely glad to see us, that I actually *relaxed*. And as soon as she'd finished fussing over us, Eve's husband Brooks broke through the small crowd gathered in the foyer to approach us with outstretched arms. "Arthur! Dennis!" he said with avuncular enthusiasm. "How wonderful to see you again!"

It really felt like we were *just* the people he'd been waiting to see all night.

"You *will* excuse me for stealing Arthur away for a moment, won't you?" he said to Dennis as he deftly linked his arm to mine. "Eve gave me explicit instructions to bring this gentleman to her as soon as I spotted him."

Before Brooks lead me away, I watched Dennis and Lillie exchange meaningful glances. They probably thought the lamb was being neatly delivered to the slaughter, but I was actually relieved to have Brooks act as my escort. I'd been worried that I would have to wait in line to speak to Eve.

She was in the living room, prominently on display in an enormous armchair a foot or so away from a picture window overlooking Central Park West. Scott Evans was sitting on the floor at her feet, drinking in every word of whatever story she was sharing with him.

"Here he is!" announced Brooks, as he ever-so-gently pushed me toward his wife's chair.

Scott jumped up to shake my hand and then both he and Brooks made themselves scarce. Eve smiled at me rather coquettishly, and, without saying a word, turned her head to the side and tapped her finger against her exposed cheek.

I kissed her on this targeted spot.

"That will have to do for now, young man," she said. "I'm still getting over the cold I came down with right after you boys left my house. Which one of you should I blame?"

"Not me! I feel great!" I assured her.

"Wonderful! That must explain how you were able to come up with the rewrites so quickly."

"Oh, good. You got them."

"Yes, John dropped them by yesterday. Of course I haven't had time to read them yet; there's just so much to do . . . "

"Sure, of course."

"But I did want to thank you for all your hard work."

"Well, I hope you—"

"Did you see the cake?"

"The cake?"

"In the dining room, you can't miss it. Oh, you must see the cake! Go!"

Having received my orders, I marched off to "see the cake."

I was disappointed she hadn't read the revisions, but was at that moment fairly confident she'd be satisfied with them. It surprised me how much I was now looking forward to getting her approval—not just for the sake of the production, but because I really wanted Eve herself to like them—and to like *me*.

Oh, well. At least she'd let me kiss her this time. It was a start.

The cake, by the way, took up most of the dining room table and was indeed a must-see. It had a chocolate mousse filling (another allusion to *Rosemary's Baby*—specifically the drugged dessert Minnie Castevet presents to Rosemary to get her ready to mate with the Devil), and had a top layer decorated with a marzipan *Moose Murders* logo. It tasted as good as it looked, and I'm happy to report that there was no—as the hapless Rosemary observed—"chalky undertaste."

A number of guests were here in the "cake room" with me, most of whom I hadn't met. We hadn't been given name tags, which was just as well since there's nothing more awkward for a tall guy like me than having to bend way down to read little messages taped on the bosoms of total strangers. I'd lost both Dennis and Brooks and knew I should mingle, but I was lousy at mingling, and—to make matters worse—all these people were already heavily engaged in conversations, which meant I'd have to be rude and break in. I started to panic again, and did my best to hide it by wandering around *intensely* studying the various moose curios hanging on the walls. A woman wearing bright canary boots was standing in front of a large rendering of the *Moose Murders* set design. She was being profusely complimented by another woman I didn't know, so I jumped to what appeared to be a logical conclusion.

"I love your work—it's a gorgeous set," I said, offering my hand to the woman in the canary boots.

"Thanks, honey. You should tell *her* that," said Betty Lee Hunt, our press rep. "Marj," she then said to the woman standing beside her, "here's another fan . . . and he's so tall!"

With help from my new best friend, Betty Lee, I managed to have a nice chat with our set designer Marjory Kellogg about her recent excursion to the Adirondack Mountains to research the region's rustic architecture. She'd captured every nuance in her design for the play's "Wild Moose Lodge," and had even incorporated several layered forest backdrops with hanging branches, and a pipe for "rain" that ran the entire length of the stage. "I don't remember the last time I had so much fun with a project," she told me.

Everybody, in fact, seemed to be having fun this afternoon. I remember thinking how much fun I'd be having, too, if only I could somehow manage to watch this all happen on closed circuit TV in the seclusion of my own apartment. I guess it was the unrelenting personal involvement that was stressing me out, but, hey, I'd get used to it.

"We're your friends, Rosemary. There's nothing to be scared about. Honest and truly there isn't!"

After a few more attempts at socializing—none particularly successful because I was feeling bigger, gawkier, and more like a total dork by the second—I headed over to the bar. While waiting my turn, I watched Mara Hobel, a perfect little lady in her black velvet skirt and white silk blouse, graciously approach the costume designer, John Sullivan. "Excuse me," she said to him. "I don't believe we've had the pleasure. I'm Mara!"

"Jesus," I thought. "If a twelve-year-old can do this, what the fuck is my problem?"

Of course, having just finished a TV movie that was probably going to be developed into a series, little Mara had more reason to be at ease than most of us.

I got the bartender's attention and ordered a screw driver. "I know that drink!" exclaimed Mara, flashing a proud grin. "It's a vodka martini with orange juice."

"And what are you having?" I asked.

"It's a Shirley Temple," she sighed, showing me her glass and losing the grin. "What else, right?"

Shortly after I'd chugged down my second screw driver, Lillie called us all into a large room where the caterers were just finishing up loading a buffet with an exquisitely prepared selection of fish, fowl, and beast— everything except moose, thank God.

Several tables had been set up cafe-style in this room. Once I'd filled my plate with a little bit of everything offered, I took my seat next to Dennis at the table reserved for the producers, Eve, Brooks, and June. There was one other empty place setting with Nick Hormann's name printed on a placard.

"So where's Nelson?" I asked John.

"He made a brief appearance earlier," John told me. "You missed him."

"He's so sexy," commented June. "I don't know—whatever he's selling, I'm buyin'. How about it, Eve? You with me on that?"

"What, dear?"

"Nick Hormann!"

"June wants to know if the young man playing your son-in-law is your *type*," explained Brooks.

"Ah! He's a good looking man, yes." Eve said thoughtfully. "Of course, he's no Jeff Chandler."

"Now, Eve," chuckled Brooks. "I'm sure most of these youngsters have no idea who that is."

Many of us at this table did know, in fact, that Jeff Chandler had played Mr. Boynton, the biology teacher who was the object of Eve's affection on the *Our Miss Brooks* radio program. She seemed genuinely surprised and flattered when we told her so.

"They thought he was too macho for television, so they replaced him," she said. "Can you imagine?"

"Since when do you get canned for being too big a hunk?" June asked.

"Philip Boynton was a very shy character," Eve reflected. "Jeff didn't look . . . shy."

"Not in the *least,*" agreed Brooks. He caught my eye and winked.

June took over as our table's moderator from this point on, expertly getting Eve to reveal a number of highlights from her professional past—some dating even before *Mildred Pierce*—that's just how good June was at this. As soon as Eve finished with one question, she'd be tossed another—and she answered most of them with poise and good humor. I noticed, while simultaneously enjoying this interview and stuffing my face, that Eve had put very little on her own plate. She rarely interrupted the flow of her speech to either chew or swallow. This was fortunate for all her avid listeners—including Scott Evans. Once or twice I glanced over at his adjoining table and watched him leaning forward in a desperate attempt to catch every word coming out of Eve's mouth. The guy was either truly star struck or taking his role as Stinky very, very seriously.

After dinner, a number of us crowded around Eve and Brooks in the foyer to say our goodbyes. John and I weren't quite quick enough to catch her attention, and she was halfway out the door before Brooks grabbed hold of her shoulders and, as though she were a mannequin, turned her body around to face us again.

"We'll see you on Sunday for the press brunch," John reminded her, "and then bright and early Monday morning for the readthrough."

"The grapefruit?" asked Eve, looking terribly confused. "We're having a *grapefruit* on Monday? Is that a custom now?"

"No, no. *Readthrough,*" John said. "We'll be reading through the play at Monday's rehearsal. But I can order you a grapefruit if you'd like."

"No, but thank you." Eve pretended to adjust an imaginary hearing aid. "Never order by mail," she advised. "Grapefruit! Ha, ha, ha!"

Dennis and I stayed behind after everyone left, to join John, Lillie, Ricka, and her husband Albert in the living room. I still hadn't come down from my two cocktails and the bottomless glass of white wine at dinner, so I was feeling just fine. John and Lillie had spared no expense and thrown one hell of a party.

It followed that they'd be putting on one hell of a show.

There really wasn't anything to worry about. I was not reliving the climax of *Rosemary's Baby*, after all. This was the Dakota, not the Bramford; John and Lillie and their coterie of investors were not witches, and I certainly was not the clueless Rosemary.

No, my unborn baby Moose was *not* destined to be the son of Satan.

Albert popped open a fresh bottle of champagne, and the six of us raised our glasses in a toast to the New Year.

"To 1983!"

"The year one."

On New Year's Eve the following night, Dennis and I hosted our own gathering for the members of our immediate "family"— Jane, Marc, and another college chum, Sally Flynn. I barely recognized Marc these days. He'd kept his vow and had quit smoking cold turkey the day after callbacks, but had also come down with a fever and suffered through a long spell of horrible headaches and nausea. While recuperating at his parents' house in Westchester these past few weeks, he'd visited the local hair salon and had allowed the stylist to talk him into getting an "image-changing" perm. The results weren't quite what he'd had in mind.

"I thought I might look like Christopher Atkins in *The Blue Lagoon*," he lamented. "Instead it came out Art Garfunkel."

That comparison was dead on, and I tried not to take all the credit for either his new coif or the post-audition depression that had apparently inspired it. I focused instead on the noisemakers, streamers, and helium-filled balloons we'd bought for the occasion. This wasn't the Dakota, but it sure was festive. We even had shiny "Disco" cups.

Jane stayed over that evening, and eventually changed into my "big and tall" thermal nightshirt with the sporty Alaskan moose logo. She and I sat chain-smoking in front of a roaring air purifier at one end of the apartment while Dennis retreated to the other, doing his best not to be asphyxiated.

"I'm worried that our relationship has no remaining perimeters," Jane confessed, as she took a long drag from her current cigarette, executed a particularly dramatic French inhale, and modestly tried to stretch her moose shirt over her knees.

After Jane had fallen asleep on the couch, Dennis and I gathered all the balloons and headed on up to the roof of the apartment. Standing on the ledge overlooking Astor Place, we ceremoniously released each of them into the cloudless night sky. Several hours had passed since they'd been injected with helium, so they were all pretty damn limp. We watched as they slowly drifted one by one onto the streets below, where they were generally ignored by most of the early-morning revelers. As luck would have it, though, our favorite neighborhood bum turned up just in time to catch the last two. After deflating them and ripping them both apart to carefully check for hidden booty, he tossed the colorful remains aside and crossed the street to investigate a more promising-looking trash bin.

"I guess this is just another one of those magical New York moments we'll remember all our lives" observed Dennis.

And he was right.

Sunday's press brunch was held appropriately enough at the restaurant Mildred Pierce on West 46th Street. This was my first experience with the paparazzi—the place was teeming with photographers and reporters, all of them behaving quite civilly when Dennis and I arrived. Truth be told, they were all noticeably bored, since our star had yet to make her appearance, and there wasn't much Betty Lee could say about the rest of us that would have made much of an impression on any of them. John and Lillie were taking up the slack, and I heard a lot of questions about "oil wells" and "cattle ranches"—which I knew was not a topic our director and as-yet-undisclosed producer was at all comfortable talking about.

When she finally did make her entrance, Eve more than made up for the wait she'd imposed on us all. She was spectacular in her white satin turban (the first of many she'd be modeling for us in the weeks to come), and was warmer, more charismatic, and more open than ever before. Of course, I'd never really seen her in this sort of arena before, and I'd probably underestimated her enormous public appeal. The press people were now so wildly attentive I wouldn't have been surprised if they'd all fallen into line and welcomed her back to Broadway with some eponymous Jerry Herman-style chorus number.

Her exuberance was infectious, and I was easily able to kid around with her this afternoon. While the two of us stood hugging each other for a photograph, somebody pinched my butt.

"Did you just goose me?" I asked, still smiling for the camera.

"Why, no!" she said. "You were goosed?"

"Uh huh."

"Well nobody goosed *me*," she pouted. "Here, trade places with me!"

And so we did, like ham actors. It was great being silly with her. Just *great*.

It was about this time that one of the photographers decided it would be fun to have Mara revisit her role as Christina Crawford. He handed her a Joan Crawford doll (the restaurant came equipped with replicas of all the characters from *Mildred Pierce*, including one of Eve as "Ida") and instructed her to abuse it in a number of inventive ways. "Punch it in the stomach!" he suggested. "That's good!" *Click.* "Now smash it against the bar! That's it! 'No wire hangers, ever!' Perfect!" *Click. Click. Click.*

"I don't know how you feel," said June, who had joined us to watch this spectacle. "But if I had a kid, I would never put her in the business. It's awful—they sacrifice being kids."

"Does Joan's head come off? Yeah? Great! Okay, why don't you strangle it first—that's good, yeah—keep strangling, strangling, good. Now twist the head right off that sucker! 'Atta girl!" *Click.*

"My friend René Auberjonois let his six-year-old son make the decision for himself," continued June. "And he chose to stay a kid."

"Hey, Miss Gable!" called the photographer. "Can we get a reaction shot from you while Mara stabs Joan Crawford with a butter knife?"

"Whattaya gonna do?" shrugged June as she left us to do her shoot.

"Personally," Eve confided as we watched June throw back her arms and contort her face in horror as Mara butchered the doll, "I'm glad Mara's mother doesn't share June's conviction."

Eve and I parted company soon after this to take our seats at separate tables; Eve was assigned the "Eve Arden," and I joined Dennis, Scott, Lisa, and the costume designer John Sullivan at the "Butterfly McQueen." There was yet another empty space set aside for Nick at this table—it was matinee day for *The Dining Room*, so once again we'd be missing his company.

"I bet he doesn't even exist," grumbled Dennis.

"Well, then, you'd better start learning Nelson's lines," I said.

Since John Sullivan was sharing our table, the "Butterfly McQueens" were the first group to inspect his portfolio of costume designs. Most of them were serviceable; one or two were better than that, verging on good. But unlike Marj's work, John's lacked any sense of fun or whimsy. I particularly objected to the skimpy cocktail dress he'd sketched out for June. Snooks was trashy, crude, and a whole lot more, but she wasn't a slut. That's not where I wanted to go with her, anyway, and I was fairly certain John (Roach) would agree. But I decided to save my critique until I'd had a chance to see June model the fully realized design.

Note to all newbie playwrights: if a costume doesn't fit what you have in mind for one of your characters, don't wait until after all the patterns have been cut and all the hemlines have been sewn before finally saying so.

The one truly inspirational outfit in John's collection was the floor-length evening gown he'd created for Nurse Dagmar, which featured a heart-shaped cutout in the back. This one was a real show stopper, and Lisa understandably touted this fact to all those less fortunate with their own costumes.

Nobody lingered over lunch. The group was quick to disperse once the photographers had gotten some final "homecoming" shots of Eve and a few more outlandish pictures of Mara committing brutal and unnatural acts on the Joan Crawford doll. God only knew when or where these photos would be printed, but that hardly mattered right now. There had been enough parties for the time being, and we were all eager to get down to business.

And because Eve and I had finally managed to break the ice, I could tell we'd be having one damn fine grapefruit tomorrow morning.

Chapter Six:

Mental Blocking

The Minskoff rehearsal complex took up 14,000 square feet in the Astor Plaza building on Broadway between West 44th and 45th streets. Its third-floor studios (two of which we'd rented for *Moose Murders*) were in continuous use for rehearsals and auditions for Broadway shows right up until a 150 percent rent increase forced the owners to shut it down in 1989. Our main room faced the New York Times building on 44th Street, and we often imagined Frank Rich sitting there with his binoculars, à la Jimmy Stewart in Hitchcock's *Rear Window*, spying on our every move. At the beginning, at least, we were happy to keep the blinds wide open.

Anthony Newley was in the studio right next door to ours, working on his musical *Chaplin*, for which he'd written the book, music, and lyrics. Unlike *Moose Murders*, *Chaplin* never made it to Broadway—Newley had the presence of mind to cancel those plans after a loss of four million dollars on the road, and an opening to lousy reviews in Los Angeles. I'm delighted to report that *Moose Murders* never lost a dime on "developmental productions."

"This is a black comedy," said John when the cast had settled down with their coffee and fruit juice that first morning. He then elaborated on his decision to embrace what he referred to as *selective realism*: "The blackness is in the lines—you don't have to go crazy to reinforce it."

Almost everybody listened to this advice—for the first readthrough, anyway. Seated on a stool and with the script securely in her hands, Eve was confident and commanding, leaving no doubt that she was the focal point of the show. As she had instructed, I'd converted most of her dialogue to zippy one-liners, and she fired them all off effortlessly. The whole thing seemed positively tailor-made for her, probably because it *had* been.

June stayed uncustomarily low-keyed throughout the reading, apparently doing her best to follow John's instructions. She was so subdued, in fact, that a comment she made during a break caught me off guard.

"My friend Alice Drummond," she said, "thinks Snooks should be a platinum blonde with black roots trying to be Joey Heatherton."

I told her I'd envisioned Snooks as a brunette, and a little *frumpier*.

"Oh, yeah?," she said, with far less intrigue than surprise. "Did you see the design for my costume?"

She had an excellent point, and once again I made a mental note to have a chat with the costume designer.

So many things to do.

Nick Hormann turned out to be a true gentleman, with an unassuming, amicable demeanor and a resonate, soothing voice. I knew even then that his was the sketchiest role I'd created, most likely because the plot of *Moose Murders* (and yes, there *was* one; be still) hinged on keeping Nelson's intimate and Machiavellian relationship with three of the female characters a great big secret. I knew I wanted him to be an *enigma*, but I hadn't really thought things out beyond that. This laziness on my part as a writer may explain, if not make any less shallow or condonable, the only remark about Nick I made in my journal after that first rehearsal: "big nose."

June, incidentally, had noticed more than Nick's nose, as she confessed to me days later.

"Don't you just want to take the zipper on his pants in your teeth," she said, "and slowly pull it down over that great big bulge?"

June often made me feel and react like a Catholic schoolboy.

Lillie was one of the very few not to follow her husband's advice for the readthrough. As the wife of the director, I imagine she thought she had a lot to prove that morning. That gave her an affinity with Lauraine, Hedda's continually ridiculed and marginalized eldest daughter. The resulting overly zealous and painfully tenacious interpretation was strangely effective.

John's blocking that first week also surprised me favorably. Although too static for my taste in Act One, it became far more involved and imaginative in Act Two. When I asked him about his approach, he told me he liked to begin with clear pictures in his mind of where he wanted each of the characters to end up logistically. He then wanted the actors to feel free to assist in getting to these locations, or "set-ups." That way the play would become a "shared event."

This sounded somewhat *gestalt* to me, but I also thought it might just be a smart way to handle this kind of black comedy. And we certainly had a group of actors willing to share their ideas.

My favorite of which that first week was Nurse Dagmar.

Lisa had an inexhaustible supply of stage bits, and I was convinced that her future reputation for this role would be nothing less than iconic. One day she would walk up to Nelson, plant her hand on a chair for support, and then nonchalantly hoist her leg around his neck, never once breaking her concentration. Another day she'd crawl out from behind the "bar" (represented by masking tape at this point) with a cigarette dangling from the side of her mouth. She would belch ever so elegantly in Joe Buffalo Dance's face. She would stand directly behind the diminutive Don Potter as Howie while he confessed to some illicit hanky-panky, vicariously reliving the details herself and mouthing the words "Do it, do it."

I truly believe that Lisa's infectious sense of fun and playfulness helped Miss Arden loosen up and relax into her own role.

I remember one time in particular when Eve affectionately patted Lisa on her behind after successfully abating one of Dagmar's chronic screaming fits. Lisa, not to be outdone, glanced down at her butt and then said to Eve in a very earnest and sultry voice: "*Thank* you."

The littlest Holloways acted like well-behaved children this first week. Mara came in already having every single one of her lines down cold and, when not on stage, she would quietly sit off to the side being homeschooled by her mother. Scott continued to be unafraid to maul and pet Eve whether or not the script called for it. At first, Eve would train her eyes on John as if to say "you *will* be putting a stop to this soon, won't you?" But it wasn't long before she warmed up to both Scott and his molestations. Outside of rehearsal, Scott kept to himself for the most part, seeking out only Eve during breaks to pump her for more Tales from Hollywood. And don't let my sarcasm fool you, here. Throughout the week Eve and I remained only distantly cordial. I just knew Scott was getting the scoop on a lot more folks than Benay fuckin' *Venuta*, and I was insanely jealous.

My relationship with the star took another change for the worse that Thursday afternoon. We were purposefully postponing work on what we referred to as Eve's "transitional scene" near the end of the play—what I suppose you might call the *denouement*, if you really want to attribute such a disciplined structural device to this play. Here's where Hedda reveals both her romantic interest in her son-in-law Nelson as well as her role as the true mastermind behind all the "moose" murders. It was verbally and physically demanding, and the one scene Eve had never really come to terms with, even after my hefty rewrites. John, understandably, had been avoiding it like the plague.

Friday morning we would finally tackle this killer scene, and John was prepared to devote the entire day to it if he had to. After the morning rehearsal on Thursday, Eve pulled me aside.

"What are your plans for lunch, son?" she asked.

I was thrilled! And Scott wasn't even around, so it looked as if I'd be enjoying Miss Arden's company all to myself.

"We need to go over that . . . *scene.*" she continued, making the word "scene" sound like something she needed to scrape off her shoe.

"I'm free," I said. "You want to go to Charleys or Barrymore's?"

"I think we'd get a lot more done if we stayed right here," she said. "If you're a good boy, it shouldn't take too long, and you'll still have time to grab a bite somewhere."

The emphasis on *you'll* wasn't lost on me. Scott was probably already at Barrymore's, reserving their usual table for two.

So Eve and I sat down with our scripts and went over that *scene* line by line. This time she didn't bother suggesting changes. She'd already cut, edited, and rewritten when necessary all on her own. She seemed genuinely shocked whenever I attempted to butt in, as though after the previous discussion with John, and my subsequent revisions, my unconditional acquiescence was now contractually understood.

My nose was so out of joint after this session I was probably permanently disfigured. And it wasn't as if she hadn't come up with good ideas, either. She *had*, and I knew it. By now she'd become very caught up in the show, and had a good handle on her character and how best to sell this final, crucial scene to the audience. The trouble was she wanted to sell it as Eve Arden, *not* Hedda Holloway—which would have been fine for something like *Hellzapoppin'* or *Sugar Babies*, I suppose. In fact, we might all have been better off if we'd simply gone ahead and jobbed in Mickey Rooney to play Nelson and added some brassy burlesque numbers—but this vision totally escaped me then. At that moment I felt patronized, pulverized, and pissed—very, very pissed.

And it showed. I did some serious pouting. But that was the extent of my aggression; I maturely accepted all her changes by muttering something like "fine, do whatever the hell you want," trudged out of the Minskoff like Eeyore, and decided to take the rest of the day off. Obviously I wasn't needed here.

"At least you *can* leave," said Dennis at home later that evening after I attempted to engage him in a pity party. "I have no lines, but I have to sit there like a fool the whole day, anyway. I'm nothing more than a living prop. I don't even have to learn blocking; wherever I'm going, somebody wheels me there. I'm bored out of my fucking mind!"

Things were tough all over, I guess.

I toyed with the idea of staying home the next morning, too, but my curiosity got the better of me. Besides, when everything fell apart (as it was *bound* to, I just knew), I'd need to be on hand with my needle and thread to stitch the Moose back together again.

No such luck. Not only were Nick and Eve both at the top of their games, but each and every one of Eve's edits worked–sometimes brilliantly. She even threw in some business right there on the spot–including a nice little red herring of a moment that cleverly suggested to the audience that Sidney might still have some life in him, and just might be capable of foiling Hedda's plans yet. She was so excited about this contribution that she insisted John call in all the other actors to watch it played out. He did, and they loved it. His "shared event" directorial concept was finally paying off.

Eve was so damn cute during all of this that, try as I might, I just couldn't keep that chip on my shoulder. She was finally having fun—just as Brooks and Glenn had promised she would, so many weeks ago. And there was no question that she had now succeeded in making a bid to own the play herself.

I decided to be magnanimous and share it with her.

We broke for lunch in great moods, all of us. This would have been the perfect moment to make amends with Eve, but, unfortunately, Dennis and I had already promised this time to Don, who wanted to discuss the role of Howie "in depth."

We ended up at Charleys, across the station from Eve and Scott. Don began by telling us how all his friends had read the script and agreed unanimously that he was Howie. Most of the conversation, however, dealt with Don Potter himself: his house and lover in Los Angeles, his vaudeville act, his age (just turned fifty), the delight his parents had experienced by his landing this job, his eternal optimism. "I know it's a cliché," he said, "but there really are *no* people like show people."

Shortly after making this pronouncement, he nearly fell off his chair greeting a conductor friend who was passing by our table. I noticed that this small commotion had caught Eve's attention, and I used the opportunity to make some sort of contact with her. I waved, idiotically. She waved back, and then blew me a kiss. Aha! We were friends!

Or at least civil acquaintances.

Things were good. There was a full runthrough after lunch, and, with very few exceptions, everything continued to flow smoothly. Afterwards John congratulated the entire cast for a "remarkable" first week, encouraged them all to get some rest over the weekend, and reminded them that they were all to be "off book" for Monday morning's rehearsal of Act One.

"Off book."

He *had* to press our luck.

Let's just start by admitting that being "off book" as early as possible is of critical importance to the success of a farce. You've got doors to slam, costumes to change, weapons to shoot, hurl, or discharge, and people to chase from one end of the stage to the other. The last impediment you need is the script in your hand. And the dialogue—whatever else you may say about it—had better come when and where it's supposed to. One flub, one missed cue, and you set off a domino effect of collateral damage that's impossible to recover from. You just can't afford to tap dance your way through a farce.

Unless, of course, you're Mara Hobel.

Ironically enough, Mara was the only cast member completely off book from day one. The rest of the group took that first week to learn their lines while simultaneously learning their blocking. The play had become cumbersome with blocking at this point, including an inordinate number of added interjections and exclamations ("Look out!," "Over there!" "Ow!" "Duck!")—all of which had to be coordinated and executed with painful precision and lightning speed. If you give the audience a moment to think–even in a *good* farce–it's death, pure and simple, cut and dry, over and out.

There are so many opportunities to fuck up something like this—even under the best of conditions.

Which is exactly why I was more than willing to give Eve the benefit of the doubt as she struggled—sometimes heroically—to keep up with the others throughout that second week. For the first few days, she refused to rehearse without her script in her hands, or in one hand, or tucked securely under her arm. She'd obviously at least attempted memorization, and would, from time to time, keep her eyes off the page and focused on whichever character or characters she was speaking to.

But, more often than not, if she wasn't reading from the script, the lines just wouldn't come. At first this was rather endearing; she had a particularly comical sound she'd make on these occasions that cracked us up— the first few times. It was a deep, long bellow similar to that made by a foghorn.

"Unnnnnnnnnnhhhhhhhhhhhhhhhh."

She'd do this while staring straight ahead. Then she'd pause, turn her head in another direction, and bellow again.

"Unnnnnnnnnnhhhhhhhhhhhhhhhh."

"She's signaling the other ships," Ricka whispered to me one time. "Storm's ahead."

We kept waiting for her eyes to light up and cast oscillating beams across the room.

By the end of the week, John insisted (nicely) that she try leaving the script behind. Perhaps, like Dumbo the Flying Elephant, she'd realize she could stay aloft without clinging to this magic feather with her Isotonered trunk.

What we got was Operation Dumbo *Drop*.

The foghorn was on loud and steady as ever, and when she wasn't bellowing, the strangest words were coming out of her mouth. Stranger even than the words I'd written for her, which, though many would argue might have been all for the better, wasn't providing much help for her fellow cast members, listening carefully for their cues. Despite Eve's frequent "warnings," the other ships were crashing and splintering against the shoals, one by one.

Nearly in tears, Eve came over to me afterwards. She patted my shoulder and said, "I apologize, son. I've just never had this problem. I'm beginning to think I may just have to learn these lines by *rote!*"

It was a heartbreaking moment, and I felt miserably inept and phony as hell as I tried to comfort her by saying things like "it's no big deal," and "it'll all work out." What I was thinking was the exact opposite: This was a *very* big deal, and things were definitely not working out.

"By *rote?*" I thought. "How else did she expect to learn her lines? By telepathy? By deep, fervent hope? By *osmosis?*"

In fact, yes—soaking up lines had been quite easy for Eve in her younger days, on the few occasions when she hadn't had the luxury of cue cards to bail her out. As it was, she was playing *Moose Murders* as if it were a *Bob Hope Christmas Special*, where all that's required is to stand still and read quips off a teleprompter. She was horribly distressed and becoming more so by the minute. As a result, John, Ricka, and Lillie all began to talk about extending previews and even taking such drastic measures as hiring an on-stage prompter or sewing a radio feed into each of Eve's turbans.

One of the worst moments came when somebody circulated an Associated Press photo taken at the *Mildred Pierce* press luncheon, where Eve was looking straight at the camera while proudly pointing her thumb at a portrait of Joan Crawford behind her. The caption underneath this piece of company contraband read:

"Line?"

Brooks swore to me that he had been faithfully running lines with Eve every night at the Wyndham, but I had trouble buying that story. Brooks was as bored as Dennis. Eve herself had often bemoaned the fact that her husband was all too eager to "play" after feverishly inventing things to keep himself busy all day during rehearsals. "So we'll go out," she'd say, "have a bite, and . . . you know." Here she'd pantomime knocking down a few. "After that," she'd say, "it's toddle on home and . . . ." Here she'd drop her head and make snoring sounds.

Dennis itched to take a crack at Eve's problem himself. He was convinced we were all just a pack of suck-ups, and that what Eve needed was a little old-fashioned discipline. "Better yet," he said, "we should have Mara's mother take over. Have Eve join Mara's homeschool sessions. And keep her there until she's learned every fucking line. If nobody wants to play 'Daddy,' then let's have 'Mommy' handle this!"

One night Dennis returned from rehearsal and confided that although he continually laughed at the bits all the actors threw in regularly from day to day as he sat watching them rehearse, he sometimes wondered about the general effect of the play as a whole. How will all this nonsense play to an outsider?

"You mean an audience," I said.

He nodded. As a full-time captive observer, he had some other questions, too: Was John aware of the play conceptually? Were there gaping holes in logic? Was anybody watching the store or just gorging on penny candy?

He said he'd chatted briefly with June about this, who'd told him, "You know, my friend Orson Bean didn't want me to do this play. He didn't think it worked."

"I think I should try to prepare us both for divergent reactions," Dennis said. "There's a lot of rah-rah team zeal that tends to make certain truths a little opaque, you know?"

I said, "Yeah, I know."

"I just hope that someone is remaining objective…" he said.

"And I don't think it's you or John" he also said.

After that little heart-to-heart, I became defensive and withdrawn, and we had quite a row. The end result was a discussion of the play's ending and my discovery—not for the first time—that a large portion of it was indecipherably convoluted. Try as I might, I couldn't remember the airtight logic I just knew I'd found when it was first written. I began to panic. This, I thought, was the sort of discussion I should have had with John before rehearsals even began.

In John's defense, Dennis also told me that our director had prefaced this last runthrough with an order to all the actors to keep on top of the cues. "No business between lines—keep it at a clip." This was an essential element of farce I hadn't been entirely certain John subscribed to. With Eve's lines down, I rationalized, we should soon be getting some fabulous results. All of the other actors, after all, were each continuing to grow in his or her own way.

Nursing my wounded pride, I stayed away from the rehearsal on Saturday. Dennis phoned to report that a miracle had evidently occurred overnight, and Eve had most of her lines down for Act One—as written, in fact. "And get this," he said. "She's even begun to *act*! I think it's safe to say she now has a vague awareness of what's going on in the play!"

"What makes you think that," I said.

"Because afterwards she told me, 'you know, I think Hedda should be more dignified at the beginning.'"

Eve lit up every time an opportunity became available for her to contribute something to the show other than memorized lines. One of the reasons Friday's runthrough had been so rough was that it had come after a taping of the radio spots, and Eve had rushed to the studio early in the morning. Once there, she'd carefully gone over the copy and decided that it gave too much away. Rather than "There goes my daughter!" after the gunshot, for instance, shouldn't it be "Could that be my daughter?" She cheerfully rewrote all of the ad copy in this fashion. She was right on the mark, too, and became eager to boast of this improvement. You could see how proud she was of her gift to the promotional campaign.

Her star's vanity was ever present. Despite its figurative connotation, the line "I didn't want you to soil those lovely hands" had to be struck. Eve was adamant that no attention ever be drawn to her hands—especially when uncovered by her gloves. Little by little, however, as she began to take ownership of the project, she began to let her hair down—quite literally, in fact. My heart skipped a beat the day she came flouncing into rehearsal without a turban, proudly sporting what very well might have been her own perky red hair—the current Arden insignia.

She remained nervous about televised interviews so we had to wait until we moved into the theater before allowing *Entertainment Tonight* to bring their cameras to a rehearsal. Although she seemed to be adjusting to the hectic pace outside of the Minskoff, she still had some classic absent-minded moments. Once, while Cliff, the assistant stage manager, was escorting her to her limo, the two were accosted by a woman asking the location of the Golden Theater. Cliff claimed not to know, and then watched the lady's jaw drop as she recognized the person he was standing next to. "Are you Eve Arden?" gasped the lady. Eve turned to Cliff and stared blankly. After a dead moment or two, Cliff finally said, "Yes! You're Eve Arden! Now get in the car!"

I sometimes wonder what would have happened if somebody—anybody—had taken off the Isotoners and slapped Eve around a little.

Just a little; don't get excited.

If we weren't being cloyingly deferential, we were throwing around cryptically backhanded compliments. Sarcasm may be the lowest form of humor, but I don't think it's particularly useful as an aide memoire.

See, it was about balls. Nobody having any, I mean. Except maybe Ricka, who finally sent Sue Henry to Eve's hotel room on a nightly basis to run lines. But Sue was at the mercy of Brooks, who apparently had a hundred ways to excuse his wife from any hard-core study each and every time Sue showed up. Eve never really improved for very long, and this remained the elephant in the room right up until the first preview.

I hope that doesn't give too much away for those of you who weren't there.

Speaking of slapping around, we actually hired a "fight master" to handle all our violence. Onstage violence, that is. His name was Kent Shelton, and if you're going to have a fight master, pick this guy . . . if he's still doing it. It certainly sounded like a James Bondian occupation, so I wasn't really surprised when Kent turned out to be a hunky matinee idol—Errol Flynn without the moustache. At the time he was working with a group performing jousts on horseback at Renaissance fairs across the country. I sometimes fantasized about being his serving wench.

Kent taught Lisa various karate stances (since, as the play's reliable device, Nurse Dagmar most assuredly was called on to kick and arm chop). I believe one of the reactionary lines I gave to Snooks was "*Chink crap, eh?"* which may give you a better understanding why many of the critics were relieved when much of the play proved ultimately inaudible.

He taught Nick how to leap from a balcony onto the back of a moose, and, as if this were not enough, he taught Mara how to stamp on feet and throw sucker punches into various unprotected crotches. Good times.

But we didn't stop at a fight master.

We brought in a choreographer, or "dance coordinator" as the union preferred to call her (Mary Jane Houdina), who worked on Mara's spontaneous tap numbers. In addition, she gave June some "cheese bits" for her act. (Talk about taking coals to Newcastle!) We also hired a music director (Ken Lundie) to help June and Don with their Singing Keenes numbers, in particular an off-key version of *Jeepers Creepers* that opened the show. Ken taught them how to be really, really bad.

That's right. We actually outsourced some of our bad.

Despite the constant problems and setbacks Eve provided by not learning her lines, I did manage to allow myself to get excited—even ecstatic—from time to time. Like when Ricka called to let me know she'd booked me my first interview. About time! I'd been wondering where the press had been hiding as I prepared for my big, auspicious Broadway debut.

I was pretty sure I was ready for Brendan Gill, Rex Reed, or even Barbara Walters.

What I got was a short and bulbous guy from *Ellery Queen's Mystery Magazine*.

I met Ricka at Sardi's to wait for him. We thought he was late, but he'd actually been there for quite some time before us, distracted by some commotion at a table around the corner involving incessantly exploding flashbulbs. Which probably meant celebrities, right? Hot cha cha! He reluctantly pulled himself away from this activity to join us.

"Something big goin' on over there," he said, and then distractedly began to ask me a series of uninspired questions. But I answered each of them professionally and eloquently, all the while trying to remember if I'd ever even seen a copy of *Ellery Queen's Mystery Magazine*. Shorty never once looked me in the eye, merely throwing me an occasional "yeah" or "go on" as he continued to strain his neck to see what was going on at the other, obviously far more *mysterious*, table.

"If he was from any reputable publication," said Ricka, once this dweeb had left to go to the john, "I'd be on the phone now telling them 'never again.'"

He eventually returned from the toilet, but I noticed he took his time creeping down the stairs. He was like a baby elephant trying to hide his telltale bulk behind a telephone pole to spy on some really cool lions and tigers.

"You know, I just don't recognize anybody over there," he said, as he scooted his chair closer to the other table to get a closer look.

"The star's right here," said Ricka coolly, pointing at me.

I loved her madly at that moment.

Fanboy soon asked me everything he cared to, and wondered if he might be able to get a couple of comps for the show.

"If I'm there to review it," he said, "it'll be in the running for an *Edgar*!" (The *Edgars* are the annual awards handed out by the Mystery Writers of America to distinguished works in the mystery genre.)

"Oh, is *that* how we get one of those?" said Ricka.

We also got a free copy of *Alfred Hitchcock's Mystery Magazine*. He was out of the other publication.

The third week of rehearsals began with my first theatrical erection. I almost feel sorry for folks like August Wilson and Neil Simon, who've watched so many marquees go up over the years they must now be totally indifferent to such ceremonies. I'd been excited a little earlier when the first quarter-page ad for the show hit the Arts & Leisure section of the *New York Times.* When Dennis and I were given our own collection of the *Moose Murders* posters that were being circulated around town (and where is this collection now, when I *really* need it), I flipped out. But none of this prepared me for the thrill of watching *hardware* that said"Moose Murders" being mounted high above the Eugene O'Neill theater. Dennis brought along his video equipment and taped our little enclave (Lillie and Marc had joined us) paying homage to this groundbreaking event.

I went back later by myself and walked by the theater several times, pretending to be a passerby getting his first gander at this upcoming spectacle. Back and forth; forth and back."Hmmmm."I remember thinking, as an innocent bystander."Looks like a new play.

"'*And* Lillie Robertson?' they say. Wonder who that is?!?"

The cast was now all off book . . . *including* Eve. She was off it, but that didn't mean she was following it. One day I read along in the script just for laughs (a little harder to come by now that we'd hit the third week), and was not surprised to discover that not one of her lines came out even remotely as written—if it came out at all. It was uncanny the way she paraphrased every stinking thought. Still, she was often rather engaging first thing in the morning. It was only after lunch and her customary glass of Chablis that we had on our hands what closely resembled a zombie in a silk turban.

On Thursday I arrived for the afternoon runthrough to discover the sidelines of the studio crammed with all sorts of people. All the designers and their assistants were there, including Kent the fight master, Ken the musical director, and Pat Collins the lighting designer. Plus many new and strange faces belonging to folks I may have never been introduced to. It was a little disconcerting, so I wasn't surprised when Ricka told me about Eve's reaction to this assemblage. She (Eve) had apparently asked Ricka to clear the room at once of all the intruders.

"You know, Eve,"Ricka reported saying,"previews begin in a little over a week. These people here today all have to see the show so they can start doing their jobs."

I squeezed into a spot between Jerry Bihm and Marj, and tried to brace myself for whatever was about to happen.

Act One soldiered on at a reasonably appropriate rate—Eve made it through with less faltering than usual. Audiences *do* help. Act Two, however, was ruinous, pure and complicated. It wasn't all Eve's fault, by any means. Several scenes had never been seriously rehearsed or even blocked, lots of new business—including chase scenes—had not been timed.

But, primarily, Eve could simply not paraphrase her way through this farcical obstacle course.

The reaction to the first act was mildly favorable. A lot of healthy laughter. A we're-with-you-all-the-way-and-it-looks-like-maybe-we'll-be-pulling-a-few-paychecks-out-of-this-sucker-after-all kind of laughter. "Gee," I thought, as I watched folks like Marj and Betty and Pat titter and guffaw, "maybe the play *does* work. Maybe it can hold up, *despite* the Mad Paraphraser."

This self-satisfaction totally deteriorated during the second act. But something prevented me from taking it out on myself, even privately. I grew angrier by the minute, glowering at everybody on the stage, and a lot of the folks in the audience, many of whom, I was quick to note, were now glowering right back. I wondered how much real effort Eve was putting into this process, and if, in fact, she realized just how dependent everyone else was on her getting it together.

I went up to her afterwards. She was just as irritable as I was, and just as distracted by our rapidly dispersing audience.

"I simply don't have enough time!" she snapped. "I finish here and go out to dinner with Brooks, have a tiny glass of wine, maybe two—and then…" She lowered her chin to suggest "beddie-bye."

I was getting to be quite good at guessing her charades.

"And the mornings!" she continued. "Why, do you know it took the girl two and a half hours to do my nails this morning?"

I struggled to be empathetic. I felt I'd accommodated this woman again and again, and had made both additions and omissions to the script when called on by her to do so. I also knew that many of her "events" had been canceled at the expense of the show's overall publicity campaign. But what really pissed me off was to hear that she still wasn't going over her lines at night, and was apparently still expecting simply to absorb the play. I knew at that moment that it wasn't ever going to happen. I felt like a caged animal.

Trouble was, I had no idea where I'd run to if somebody lifted the latch and set me free.

While I was listening to a litany of similar complaints from Eve, Jerry came over with the star's pay envelope. "For a real good job today, honey!"

he quipped. She hit him playfully on the arm (she did this a *lot*), and sighed loudly with frustration (she did that a lot, too).

I wasn't the only one pissed off. Lillie left the studio with us that evening, and began to spit venom.

"It's not the Eve Arden Fan Club anymore!" she fumed. "That woman is being paid five grand a week—you'd *think* she'd give us a little in return!"

So. It was out. Now we knew the star's salary. *Five thousand dollars*—and delivered in cash every week—which Dennis told me was an old Hollywood custom. Figured. So much of this experience had reeked of old Hollywood from the beginning.

Lillie's current tantrum was par for the course these days. Both Lord and Lady Roach had been showing us their dark sides the deeper we hacked our way inside the Moose jungle. Saturday afternoon we had lunch at Joe Allen's—already famous for its posters of infamous Broadway flops like *Kelly* and *Breakfast at Tiffany's.*

Welcome, Arthur, to the House of Fore Shadows!

Despite Eve's small improvement at that afternoon's rehearsal, Lillie was on a tear about how she felt serious advantage was being taken of all of us. Bad-mouthing Eve had become something of a cause célèbre for Lillie. I'd noticed that Ricka would often feed this particular obsession and that John would often let it go—thereby encouraging it, in my estimation. I suspected that this might very well be part of the attraction John and Lillie had for each other—her spitfire moments complimented the perpetual cool on John's part. Jane, incidentally, was convinced that John's unflagging serenity was the result of always being better off financially than his peers—that certain obligation the very rich appear to feel not to make waves, not to exploit their God-given advantage over the rest of us rabble.

It now appeared, however, that even John had his limits. He'd let everyone off for the afternoon, but not as a reward. "There's a condition," he said, actually sounding a bit forceful. "There will be no more 'memory work' on Monday. If you have your lines I can help you further. Otherwise, there's nothing more I can do."

He even dared to glance directly at Eve when he said that.

After lunch, Lillie hurried off to her first costume fitting, and John, Ricka, Dennis, and I all climbed into John's little Saab and sped out to Brooklyn to visit the scene shop where Marj's set was under construction. John's driving reflected his mood; he reminded me of Cruella DeVil chasing after all those Dalmatian puppies. We got hopelessly lost, and as Lillie's directions became less and less useful, John's passion rose and rose until Dennis and I at long last got a glimpse of the inner aggression he so adroitly concealed most of the time. Dennis mentioned this revelation to Ricka, who seemed much more interested in getting back to the city to celebrate her birthday with her husband.

The scene shop was cavernous. After trouble initially finding a suitable ingress, we walked in like the meek and mild Dorothy and her pals to genu-flect before the work of the Wizard of Design. Marj Kellogg's set—let me just tell you, folks—was and *remains* to this day the best thing about *Moose Mur-ders*. I swear she must have been hiding next door to my family's camp at Big Moose Lake in the Adirondacks. Every detail was flawless, down to the warm earthen color scheme. Dennis and I stood together and grinned like little boys; all four of us scampered about the set in unabashed delight. We climbed up the stairs, strolled across the balcony, took turns sitting at the window seat or standing on the"live entertainment"platform, came in and out of all the doors and opened all the windows, all the while admiring the enormous stone fire-place and the birch latticework and the wealth of whimsically rendered animal pelt-and-bone furnishings. I stood in the middle of this magnificent creation, raised my arms high over my head, and exclaimed,"Broadway is great!"

And I meant it. I was ready to move into that set. We all were, I think. What a wonderful break from the unspeakable stress and tension this hell-ish week had brought so far.

We all chose separate corners of our new home and sat in happy si-lence for quite some time. Finally one of us moved, and the rest reluctantly followed off the set, out of the shop, and back into the gray winter day.

We drove back to lower Manhattan to visit the costume shop. Lillie was there, modeling Lauraine's very tasteful lavender suit. Dennis was whisked away to try on his Brooks Brothers monogrammed robe and slip-pers, and became despondent over the flab he had been determined to lose before opening.

"Don't worry," encouraged John. "Body bandaging hides a multitude of sins."

John Sullivan timidly took us on a tour of the shop and we viewed most of the other completed costumes. Eve was to have three separate ensembles, including a handsome business suit and a more relaxed outfit featuring a pair of those leather pants she'd always wanted for the first act, and a Chinese affair (again per her request) for the second. All three were on display, and all were equally lovely.

The visits to both these shops had been so much fun, and so damn encouraging, that I wondered if we might possibly get away with opening the show with just the set and costumes. I mean, think about it. The audience could sit admiring all these marvelous *accoutrements* for two hours; who needed a script and actors?

Monday morning the cast was joined by the understudies, all two of them, Suzanne and Andy. (Dennis, of course, was present as always, in his "chair.") It had been my understanding that others would be hired after the opening depending on how the show was received. This went the way of other such "understandings" I'd had with John when I overheard him advising Andy which roles to learn first, now that time was of the essence.

"Howie first," he said. "Then Stinky."

Suzanne, in turn, would be responsible for all the female roles except Gay, but, as far as I knew, no plans were being made to find another little girl to take Mara's place should she choke on a chicken bone or something. Sue would learn Hedda's part only in case Eve became ill in the middle of a performance—it was presumed the star would begin each show no matter what condition she was in. The past several days had obviously taken their toll. Why throw good money after bad when your ship had already sprung a fatal leak?

I visited Marc that evening, intending to come clean about what I had learned. But, once again, I wimped out. Telling him that Scott had been cast had been hard enough. Dennis had warned me that it would be cruel to withhold this information, since Marc's life seemed once again to be on hold until he assumed the role of understudy.

"You think 'and Lillie Robertson' is bad," said Marc. "Just wait until 'for Marc Castle'" (from the dedication page) "takes over!"

Squirming a little, and trying to come off as nonchalant as possible, I asked him about his "upcoming projects."

There were none. True to his word, he'd quit smoking and (perhaps as a result) was eating a lot of Entenmann's baked goods and drinking an inordinate amount of milk—even for him. He'd dropped a recent idea of writing a book. The Equity board was bare. His unemployment benefits had been extended for another three months, but he wasn't going to worry about that.

"Why should I panic until I find out whether or not the show is going to run?" he asked.

I nodded, knowingly. I encouraged him to keep looking for some sort of diversion, and the conversation immediately turned south.

"I found a copy of the *Sunday Times* in the garbage yesterday," he mentioned, "so I finally got to see the ad."

"What?" I said, trying not to appear insulted. "You didn't rush right out to buy your *own* copy as soon as it hit the stands?"

"The border is good," said Marc. "But the moose itself could be a little more . . . zany. "

"You think?"

"Yeah. And my friend Barbara called and said 'they're not spending a lot of money on this, are they? It looks *inexpensive.*'"

It occurred to me that this would be the perfect time to hit him with my news. But I let it go. In fact, I never did tell him. Why bother? I think we both knew the subject was just about as moot as a subject of this sort could get.

Around this time we heard the first radio spot on WNCN. It was awful. Mara sounded stagey, the announcer sounded bored, and the background music was absurd—but not in a good way. There was nothing unique about it. It was dishearteningly forgettable.

To make matters worse, we had to listen to it with Dennis's mother, Mary Ann, who was visiting from Massachusetts. She'd refused to stay at a hotel, because she didn't want to miss a single second of what was going on. She was, in fact, staking her entire future on this production's success, and this lousy ad did nothing whatsoever to encourage her. She droned on and on about it, demanding to know how we could let something like this be aired in public *(Mary Ann, this is just the radio ad—wait'll you see the play!)*, and there was no place we could hide from her in that tiny apartment. Finally, to shut her up, we gave her some money and pleaded with Jane to take her out shopping for an opening night dress.

Luckily for us, Jane was in pretty decent spirits these days. She'd received a copy of the dust jacket for *Murder on Cue* with her name and a full photo on the back. Nice butch haircut, very authorish.

"Next time I'll have them shoot me with a cigarette and a glass of Scotch," she said. "Move over, Lil Hellman."

She'd been assured by the publisher that she'd have an initial sale of at least 3,000 copies to libraries, since the book would be part of the

Doubleday Crime Club. And even better, she'd just been reviewed well by *Kirkus*—they'd found the bitchiness of her main character to be a total delight and a major compensation for any lack of credibility in the story line. She had always wanted to hold her publication party backstage at whatever theater was going to house *Moose Murders*, and, with this impressive review under her belt, she now wanted to invite other show business personalities who had also doubled in the mystery-writing genre.

"Tom Tryon should be a shoo-in! "she said. "We always feature his books at Murder Inc."

"Whatever you want." I said. "Just take Mary Ann out to buy a dress. And please. Take all the time you need."

This initial outing did not go especially well. Jane took Mary Ann to a few places, but nothing was appealing, nothing fit, nothing was quite right for this most important night of all nights, past or future. It took a while to exhaust her patience, but Jane finally hit her spiritual nadir and was forced to leave Mother alone to fend for herself at Lord and Taylor's. Dejected, bitter, alone, and in tears, Mary Ann returned to the apartment only to discover that neither Dennis nor I was in any condition to console her.

The runthrough that Monday—just four days before we opened this thing to the public with our first preview—had been catastrophic. Not merely unprepared, Eve was now listless and sluggish. No command. No lines. Her final scene with Nelson came off as if she'd glanced at the script briefly for the first time only yesterday. I knew that couldn't be the case, because this was the scene she'd had me rewrite to her exact specifications. We were told later that they'd run this scene three separate times after we'd left, and that Eve still had suggestions for things to add and things to cut.

"No more," John told her. "Please learn what you *have*."

John also revealed that she had been coming to him privately throughout the rehearsal process with certain insertions or rewordings and that he had always told her to "check with Arthur."

"She stopped doing that back in Los Angeles," I reminded him.

I'd stayed home for the first part of the rehearsal on Tuesday, thinking I'd have the place to myself. Mary Ann was out continuing the great opening night dress search and I figured I'd be safe for quite some time. Not even an hour after she'd hit the streets, Mother made her triumphant return with the perfect black dress she'd picked up at a department store right there in our neighborhood.

Oh, good. We could open the show; Mary Ann had her fucking dress. But I also had this still very unhappy lady's company for the rest of the morning. Things just couldn't get any brighter.

About the same time Mary Ann turned on the TV to watch one of her "stories," the phone rang.

It was Ricka with some news to disprove my theory.

We would probably still be opening the show.

But maybe *not* with Eve Arden.

"Like sands through the hourglass," blared the TV announcer, "so are the days of our lives."

MOOSE MURDE🛏S

The official *Moose Murders* logo.
Artist: Jerry Bahl

Eve Arden poses with her Moose Murders co-star.
PHOTOGRAPH BY GERRY GOODSTEIN

Hedda and Cast. from left: Mara
Hobel, Scott Evans, Eve Arden,
and Lillie Robertson.
PHOTO BY GERRY GOODSTEIN

Hedda Holloway and her
loathsome brood. from
left: Scott Evans as Stinky,
Eve Arden as Hedda, Lillie
Robertson as Lauraine, and
(front) Mara Hobel as Gay.
PHOTO BY GERRY GOODSTEIN

"Something has gone terribly wrong." The first body is discovered. Back row (from left): Dennis Florzak, June Gable, Don Potter, Lisa McMillan, Mara Hobel, Eve Arden. Front: Nicholas Hormann, Lillie Robertson, and Scott Evans.
PHOTO BY GERRY GOODSTEIN

"I erected a tent." Nurse Dagmar and the Singing Keenes. from left: Don Potter, Lisa McMillan, June Gable.
PHOTO BY GERRY GOODSTEIN

The Wild Moose Lodge. Magnificently detailed set by Marjorie Bradley Kellogg.
PHOTO COURTESY OF MARJORIE BRADLEY KELLOGG

The Playwright
and the Star.
PHOTO BY
GERRY GOODSTEIN

The Producers and the Star.
from left: Ricka Kanter Fisher,
John Roach, Eve Arden.
PHOTO BY GERRY GOODSTEIN

Accomplices. Arthur Bicknell
and Dennis Florzak

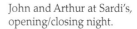
John and Arthur at Sardi's, opening/closing night.

Stepping In. Miss Arden's replacement, the intrepid Holland Taylor with Force Ten producers, Ricka and John.

moose murders

MILDRED PIERCE
345 W. 46th ST.
NEW YORK CITY

EUGENE O'NEILL THEATRE
49th Street West at B'Way
MOOSE MURDERS
Est. Price $30.00
OPENING NIGHT
ORCHESTRA
P 113

Moose paraphernalia

I wore this on the lapel of my tux, opening night. (Thanks again, Betsy Janes!)

104

"The Family." from left: Dennis Florzak, Jane Dentinger, Marc Castle, Arthur Bicknell, and Sally Flynn

The Author and his Revivalist. with John W. Borek

Arthur and the Rochester "Moosies," August, 2008.

Chapter Seven:

About All, Eve

"Here's what John has decided to do," began Ricka. "He's going to wait until after tomorrow's rehearsal. If there's no improvement, he'll ask her point blank if she has any interest in continuing this project. If she says 'no,' he'll let her go. If she says 'yes,' he'll plow through until Saturday's first preview."

"And what if the play is still a train wreck after Saturday?" I said.

"He'll ask her again."

"Brilliant."

"Yeah, but you see, *this* time, if she says 'yes,' he'll fire her anyway."

"Anything you need me to do?"

"No. We've already put feelers out to Anne Francine, Peg Murray, and Joan Copeland. Best thing to do is just sit tight."

"Okay, swell. You'll let me know if you think of something."

"Are you coming to the runthrough this afternoon?"

"Wouldn't miss it," I said. "My love to John."

I contemplated the ramifications of firing Eve Arden. Not only would it mean at least a loss of $200,000 (she would still be paid through her six month contract), but bringing in a replacement at this late date would be *death* for the play and its box office.

And not a cozy, farcical death.

I thought a lot about Eve, trying to put myself in her turban, so to speak. Was it all just too exhausting? Was it no longer physically possible to maintain the Eve Arden persona—*and* be competent—sixteen hours a day?

I managed to get Mary Ann to turn off the TV long enough so I could listen to a cassette recording of the most recent radio ad. I noted the improvement immediately. Here was the Eve Arden we'd heard all too infrequently. Varied pitch. Boundless energy. Obvious commitment. Maybe radio was the answer. Maybe we could just broadcast the play, and bring back talk radio. A pleasant image of a perfectly groomed 50s family, all gathered around the old faithful Victrola in the parlor, briefly passed through my mind: "Return with us now to the thrilling days of yesteryear! Eve Arden rides again!"

In much better spirits (who knows which level of denial I'd reached by this time?), I left Mary Ann to her soaps, and treated myself to a cab to the Minskoff. My old college chum Barbara Kerr was in town from Ohio, and we'd made plans to have her join us for the runthrough of Act Two. Unbeknownst to me, John had asked June to play everything "straight" in order to recapture the "essence" of Snooks, whatever either one of them imagined *that* to be—my own vision was long gone. The result was an almost clinically depressed Snooks, so overwhelmingly subdued she dragged everybody else down with her. I think Barbara was happy just to have been allowed into an otherwise "closed" set, but the whole thing was a real snooze. This, I must say, might have been an improvement over the usual uncontrolled mania.

"Solid performance!" said Lillie to June, afterwards.

"But I didn't *do* anything," said June.

"Yes, it was lovely," cooed Lillie.

Barbara, Dennis, and I left the studio and walked over to the O'Neill, where workers were beginning to reassemble the set on stage. We entered through the stage door and made our way to the front of the house. The basic framework was up, without any of the accoutrements—so far, only the birch bark wainscoting that lined the proscenium arch and the polished wooden floor for the "entertainment" platform had been constructed. Full-size plastic elms and pines were spread out on tarps thrown over the theater seats—all of them soon to become an Adirondack forest.

Our moods soaring, the three of us scampered up to the balcony, where we could safely admire all these strange, wonderful men who'd been employed to erect the Wild Moose Lodge on this very site.

"Oh, look who's here!" said Barbara, as Eve and Brooks suddenly appeared and began to walk across the stage below. We waved, and eventually joined them in Eve's dressing room.

Unlike the house itself, these rooms backstage were pretty bleak.

"Perhaps some posters will brighten this up." Said Eve, examining her ample dressing room and its adjoining parlor.

"How about a Chinese silk screen?" suggested Dennis.

"Yes!" agreed Eve. "Could you run out and get me one?"

We investigated the other dressing rooms, and Dennis found one especially to his liking. It had a shower.

"This is like choosing a dorm room," he said.

It really was. We wondered what it would be like to call this home for an extended period of time.

We came back out front to find Ricka, in a rage. The rest of the marquee, which was to have gone up no later than this morning, had still not arrived. The elevator in the warehouse where it had been built had a broken cable which had gone unrepaired for weeks. The stairway there was circular and the windows were too small for the marquee—the logo moosehead with a full set of antlers—to fit through. Promises were made to have all these problems solved and to have our moose beacon delivered all in one piece tomorrow morning.

We said our goodbyes to Barbara. It had been enormously gratifying to share all of this—even the occupational hazards—with a friend from the outside. We were also happy that Barbara could have this experience now—since she'd be unable to attend the opening. She had other plans. She was getting married.

"Well," she said. "Since Jane has her book and you've got your play, I figured it was the only thing that hadn't been *done!*"

The next morning—our first day in the theater—was full of magic for the first hour or so. It didn't really matter what the play was, or what kind of trouble we were having with it, today we were all rosy-cheeked school kids checking one another's accommodations. Dennis's dressing room—the one with its own shower—was on the top floor. His neighbors would be Suzanne and Andy. They'd already begun to call this floor the "understudy suite." Down a flight were rooms claimed by Lisa, Jack (who had his own shower, too), and Scott. Lisa had a window overlooking 49th street, and had brought a tacky yellow throw rug with her which she immediately threw down on the floor. She demanded that we each come to admire it, which we did, joyfully.

And-Lillie-Robertson was in the star wing with Eve. She had, I must say, begun acting the role of prima donna. She prissed, she pouted, she ordered people about.

Ah, well. A minor irritant, all things tallied.

There was a mailbox slot for each of us downstairs, and several of the cast members already found invitations from press agents to "get in touch" when they had a chance. No agent appeared interested in me, but I was just as excited to find a note from my old high school drama teacher—who'd enclosed a clipping from a play I'd done fifteen years earlier.

Wow. Fifteen years seemed like a lifetime ago . . . then.

The runthrough the day before had been good enough at least to postpone further discussions about firing Eve. I assumed that John had given her his soft-core ultimatum and that she had indeed confirmed her "interest" in staying with the project. But obviously the talk hadn't had much effect. She was still paraphrasing. Lines like "Is talking permitted?" became "Is speaking all right?" and "Have we lost all electricity?" became "Are we all out of electricity?" No big deal. When the rewording made no sense, though, it really burned my ass, because Hedda was supposed to be . . . unnnnnnnnnhhhhhhhhhhhhhhhh . . . *incisive*.

The much bigger problem was when she had clumps of words to tackle at once (I'd carefully removed anything resembling a monologue, but she still had to deliver one or two complex sentences strung together on occasion). Most of these attempts were in shambles. During a line readthrough in the basement before rehearsal, she freely confessed "I didn't have time to go over these, you know." Then, after a beat, she commanded "Arthur, leave the room!"

I did, shortly thereafter, not to behave, but because I was feeling in the way—as out of place as Brooks, in fact, who could be found wandering aimlessly throughout the hallways and alcoves all day long.

The set—all dressed, now—was awe inspiring. My circuits began to overload; I was teetering toward at least a minor breakdown (whether I was aware of it or not.) The tension was suffocating.

Dennis and I sat down together in the orchestra seats for the "get acquainted with the set" rehearsal, and it wasn't long before something set me off—it could have been oxygen at that point, who knows—and we had a verbal battle that almost incapacitated me. Dennis abruptly left his seat and disappeared into the back of the theater. I sat alone, fuming and miserable, for as long as I could—five minutes, tops, no longer.

I sought Dennis out, saw that he was still in no mood for my company, and promptly broke into tears. Before I had a chance to fill the rafters with my heaving sobs, he quietly took my arm and escorted me up to the balcony.

Only when he was sure that we were quite alone did he then administer some desperately needed TLC.

"You know I'll always be here for you," he whispered.

That I managed to hear. Worked like a charm.

Once I'd calmed down and was no longer either weeping or trembling, he left me alone to go over opening night party reservations. This was a good job for me. Not exactly mundane or mindless, mind you, but not breathtakingly exciting, either. I really was in no condition to take any more stimulation—I'd probably have been best off licking stamps or counting backwards from a zillion, or so.

Like Don Quixote facing the Knight of the Mirrors, I was coming precariously close to seeing things as they really were—in spite of all the glittering tinsel that was hanging everywhere I looked. I knew I had to get a grip. As I sat watching a dreamlike combination of splendor and messiness, I'd cower when approached by Ricka's husband, Albert, or Brooks, or John Sullivan, or anyone else. I didn't want to talk to anybody. I'm sure my eyes were glazed. There may, in fact, be such a thing as *too much*.

Picture call happened sometime while I was in this daze. Bouncy Betty Lee whipped through this process, taking barely an hour. The best shot, I saw later, was of Eve standing alone on the balcony, leaning over the centrally located and most monumental moose head. The costumes were all workable, but the one that had impressed me the most on paper—Dagmar's evening gown—turned out to be a huge disappointment. The heart-shaped cutout·on the back wasn't nearly prominent enough—you couldn't really tell it was a heart—and the body stocking underneath that John the Designer had chosen to equip her with made the whole ensemble look baggy and ill-fitting. A far departure from the intoxicating, chic, and shapely outfit we'd all been anticipating.

The set, on the other hand, was shaping up nicely. The moose heads— all three of them—were fantastic. Along with a coiled rattlesnake, a stuffed goose, and several skeletons from identifiable woodland creatures, the skull of what could only have been a unicorn held a prominent position. All the trees had left the front of the house and were now visible through the windows of the lodge. I knew the "rain machine" had been installed, and tomorrow, ironically for the first "dry tech," we would see and hear it in action—along with sound and lighting effects to create "one of this region's notoriously severe rainstorms."

The familiarization rehearsal resumed directly after the photo call, and tempers steadily began to wear dangerously thin. How much longer would June and Don be able to abide each other's attempts to steal the scenes they were sharing?

How much longer would Nick be able to put up with Lillie's insistence that the rehearsal be stopped dead in its tracks for yet another question she had for John about specific moments of self-actualization her character Lauraine may—or may *not* be experiencing at this specific moment? Probing questions that were—I needn't mention at this juncture—rarely answered to her satisfaction.

How much longer would any of the others be able to withstand the incessant clicking and clacking of little Mara's tap shoes?

Crisis hit when Eve pushed Dennis and his wheelchair into Jack, ran to get out of the way, tripped over a floorboard, and fell flat on her face. *Clunk!*—like a sack of potatoes.

Everything froze for at least three seconds—including my pulse.

As if on cue, everyone on stage came out of this trance together, and rushed to assist her. She was moving, and waving the "okay" sign.

I leaned over to Sue Henry, who had the misfortune to be sitting next to me at that moment.

"There goes the show," I whispered. "Now we'll have to shoot her."

But, as my mother used to say, *up she jumped and rubbed her bump*, and—aside from a bruised knee—appeared to be in no worse condition. She blamed her pumps for this mishap, complained that the boots she was supposed to be wearing were still being custom made.

Jerry let the actors go to lunch an hour early after this, and gave them all a little pat on the back verbally—something I wished John would do from time to time. "Say something encouraging to them," I thought. "Hell, say something discouraging—just *talk* to them!"

"I wish he'd *set* something" muttered Jerry that evening as I stood in the wings watching the runthrough.

But that wasn't John's style—it never had been. I don't really know what his style was, but it didn't include much communication with anybody on or off stage. Tonight we encountered technical problem after problem—as was to be expected when you begin to execute blocking on the real set for the first time. Through them all, John remained silent. The actors had to scream out "John!" before he'd attend to anything, and even then, he'd seldom say anything beyond "fine" in response to anything they asked. Jerry, in fact, began to direct by default. The cries for "John!" gradually changed to less frantic calls for "Jerry." They didn't have to shout for Jerry. He was right there, doing what he could.

After lunch Pat held a cue-to-cue for the lights in Act One. This went off nearly without a hitch; her talent was dovetailing Marj's. It was only when the actors were brought on stage that things began to spiral downwards once again.

"Oh, Jerry . . ." drawled Eve at one point, no longer the least bit self-conscious about interrupting the flow of the runthrough. Perhaps because there was no flow, and never had been. At this point it was barely a trickle.

"Yes. Eve?"

"Don't you think we should postpone Saturday's preview? I just don't think we're going to be ready."

"Talk to John."

"Well, every time I do, he tells me to talk to Ricka!"

"John?" called out Jerry.

"What?" came back a voice from the third row orchestra.

"Eve wants to know—"

"Just keep going. You're doing fine."

"Okay," said Jerry. "Let's take it from Eve's line, 'Tell me, where is your caravan?'"

"Fine," said John.

Eve shook her head and raised her eyebrows, then soldiered on.

"Tell me," she recited, turning to June and Don. "Where is your...*cadenza?*"

After that, she introduced her husband as Sidney *Holiday* and for some reason the rest of the cast found this so uproariously funny the rehearsal had to be stopped to allow them time to cumulatively get it together.

I remembered laughter, but I hadn't heard it like this for a while. I was now pacing back and forth in the back of the theater while chain-smoking a pack of cigarettes. Marj and Dennis joined me there at one point, and I finally had the chance to tell the designer how much I loved her set.

"We're considering contracting you to build us one of these on Big Moose Lake for real," I said.

"So," Dennis looked straight at Marj, and gestured toward the stage. "What do you think? *Still* think it's funny?"

"I think the play is very funny." said Marj. "I love the *play.*"

The rehearsal resumed, but everyone now seemed edgy as hell. Lisa and Don pulled some new business on June, and June received this by nearly pushing Don off the stage. Jack struggled to run up the stairs and across the balcony in his moose head, which virtually blinded him. Lisa cut her finger open on a moose antler, and Mara, running into a closet, slamming the door behind her, and then coming face to face with a huge blind Moose Man (only this time for *real*), burst into authentic tears and had to be comforted by her mother for quite some time. I don't know if anybody ever comforted Jack.

Through it all John remained comatose.

"This piece of business doesn't really work anymore," somebody would say.

"Fine," said John.

"There's not enough time for me to make my exit," somebody else would say.

"Fine," said John.

Several hours later we threw ourselves into a cab, and, once home, stayed up for hours rehashing everything that had gone on and trying to convince ourselves any way we could that we'd be ready for the first preview on Saturday.

Here's what I wrote in my journal that night. I think it pretty much sums up my grand delusion about this fiasco:

"We're fortunate in many respects. The play is a farce, and, as such, really directs itself."

That's right. Sort of like the Chia Pets™ that were becoming so popular that year. Just add actors, and watch your farce grow a full head of stage direction.

Here's another gem from that same journal entry:

"We're also fortunate to have an ensemble of comic professionals who can all do farce and make the whole production seem coordinated."

Note the word "seem." No play is ever *actually* coordinated, right? It only seems that way, due to the, oh, I don't know, innate magic of theater, I guess. Who needs a director? This is farce. Which is another word for free-for-all. So just go nuts, please.

And our "comic professionals" included Lillie Robertson, who was performing her frothy bits of business as if she were a principal actor in the latest Hill Cumorah Pageant.

"Dennis tells me that should we ever find ourselves in the position of dealing with Force Ten again, we must insist that John not direct and Lillie not star."

Can you see me vigorously nodding my assurance to myself as I wrote each word of that axiomatic line?

But, other than that, we're having a wonderful wine; wish it were beer.

I don't bother reserving myself a seat for this first preview. I suspect I won't be sitting still for very long. Before the performance begins, I do manage to sit for a spell with John, downstairs in the basement greenroom. We are both of us at a loss for ways to make ourselves useful. Mara skips by in her powdered-blue little sailor suit and matching bonnet, carrying an oversized lollypop—on her way to the stage for a final costume adjustment.

We listen to her clickity-clack her way up the stairs.

"She in the show?" I deadpan.

This cracks us both up, inexplicably.

Aside from the fact that I am rapidly discovering that there is no safe, comfortable place to hang out in this entire Broadway theater, what troubles me most is that a show of mine in such bad shape is about to be presented to over a thousand people. I wander into the house and somehow manage to take solace by watching all those matronly usherettes in their appropriately funereal black frocks with the starched white collars, cheerfully going about their business escorting hundreds of strangers to their seats as if this is just another opening preview to just another show.

Before I know it, the house lights dim, and I gingerly sit down in an empty aisle seat in the last row.

Seconds after this the theater becomes totally dark. A long, mournful moose bellow shakes the overhead chandeliers. The audience laughs.

So far so good.

The curtain rises to the Singing Keenes' execrable rendition of "Jeepers Creepers" already in progress. The audience seems to adore them, and gives them a burst of applause after their first exit.

Nice, nice.

Here comes Nurse Dagmar. Are they going to love her as much as the playwright does? Seems like it. Although Snooks and Howie get more response—and continue to do so once they return. Sight gags going well. Audience reaction may be getting a little tepid, now. That's okay. Eve's about to make her entrance.

Oh my God. Eve's about to make her entrance.

I cover my face with my hand and begin to watch the play through my fingers.

Nurse Dagmar opens the French doors and we get the full sound and sight effect of the rain machine. My God, that's effective! Look at it coming down! Such a downpour! Splashing and spraying on everybody and everything! And the rain is so . . . so . . . deafening.

Here now are the Holloway children: Stinky, Laurraine, and Little Gay, all huddled around their mother under her great big umbrella. The rain is crashing onto the top of the umbrella and pouring off its sides. It is Niagara. You can barely hear Eve's first line:

"Here we are children, here we are. Babies can let go, now."

What you do manage to hear is that unmistakable dipthongy delivery. Yep. That's Eve Arden, all right.

Hoots, hollers, and extended applause.

Welcome back to Broadway, Eve! We love you!

The audience stays with her as long as they can. They really do.

Howie's "blind" bits go over better than anything else—that and Stinky strangling Little Gay. Gay is despised. Mara, getting loud reactions to her shtick for the first time, begins to ham it up, indiscriminately tampering with other people's business. (Both June and Lisa will have words with the child after the show. She is still a little green about reciprocity on stage, but with Miss Gable as her mentor, I have no doubt she will have a speedy education.)

But Eve's performance is doddering, unsure, and at times sickeningly apologetic. By the end of the first act, there is no doubt where this play is going. You might be able to hear the flush above the rainfall.

The suspense of the second act, for those who choose to remain, has very little to do with the play. It is more about whether or not Miss Arden will make it to the final curtain. What I see (when I dare to look) is somebody's sweet old grandma, all dressed up for a party, who is obviously overwhelmed by all this excitement and needs to get straight to bed before she says another word or she may drop to the floor in exhaustion.

They give June the biggest response for the curtain call—perhaps more out of sympathy and appreciation of her tenacity than for anything else. The applause dies down noticeably when Eve takes her bow.

So much for deference to a living legend. This does not bode well.

"I guess they didn't believe me as a villain," she says to me after the show.

As emotionally wrecked as I am, this confession from her breaks my heart. I don't remember a darker moment than this one.

Dennis, who has spent the evening wrapped in gauze from head to foot, is not so sympathetic.

"What did you expect her to say?" he asks. "God, I sucked! Let's fire my sorry ass!"

I go outside for just a moment to say goodbye to some of my friends from Air France to whom I've given comps this evening, and find that the only way back into the theater is through the stage door. Unfortunately, this is now blocked by a swarm of autograph seekers that has already enveloped Eve and Brooks. I figure I'll squeeze by unnoticed, but am not unpleased to hear my name shouted loudly and enthusiastically by somebody in the crowd. A Playbill and pen are thrust at me; I graciously take the pen and confront my fan.

It's that jerk from Ellery Queen Mystery Magazine, *finally giving me his undivided attention.*

I smile demurely and sign my name: "Barbara Stanwyck."

The next evening, Sunday, John called a summit meeting at the Dakota. Dennis and I spent some time beforehand going through the entire script, making dozens of notes on focus and a wide range of suggested improvements. We figured it was going to be a long evening, but maybe—just maybe—we'd all be willing to be totally honest with one another for once. I didn't see the point of opening this show otherwise.

As soon as all the major players had settled in the office "board room," John gave the floor to me. I hadn't expected to be the first to talk, but figured what the hell. What have I got to lose at this point? I began to talk about all the basic elements that were missing from the show. The gaps in logic, the inept blocking, the overbearing sound of the rain machine, the lack of focus and leadership. John, Lillie, and Ricka stared back at me in shock. There was a lonnnnnnnnng pause after I'd finished. Obviously this was not what they had expected me to say, or even close to the reason we had all gathered here this evening.

Finally Lillie spoke up.

"There's only *one* culprit here," she said.

"We're tired of waiting for miracles," Ricka elaborated. "Every accommodation has been extended to Miss Arden, from the producers, from me, from each member of the cast. "

"The last scene has never worked." said John. "Part of that is my fault, yes. And part of it's yours." He glanced at me with ever-so slight admonishment.

"I've rewritten—"

"Yeah, yeah. We know. You've sliced and diced the thing. But it still isn't working."

"How much blame to dole out to either the director or the playwright is entirely beside the point," said Ricka. "Eve is exhausted by the end of the play, and has no energy to make that crucial eleventh-hour transformation. Even if she *did* know her lines."

"Which she doesn't." said Lillie. "She's totally confused out there."

"It's not fair to the rest of the cast," said John.

"The critics are not going to be kind," said Ricka. "And it's her ass on the line, too."

"Tomorrow," said John, "we're going to ask Bret Adams to watch the show." Bret, Eve's agent, was one of the biggest, most respected, and *best liked* fellows in the business. "Hopefully, Eve's feelings will be apparent to him, and he'll make it easier for her . . . and for us."

"What happens if he doesn't?" Dennis said.

"Then we'll have Eddie get in touch with both Bret and Glenn and drop the bomb. So to speak," said Ricka.

"I'll call Stuart Howard tomorrow, too," John said. "We're gonna have to find another Hedda in a hurry. When we have one, the previews will be suspended, and we'll do a week of rehearsals to work her in. That tentatively pushes the opening back to the 22nd of February."

"In the meantime," Ricka said immediately, "we resume as normal with our workthroughs. No one will be told. We're hoping she'll just step down and not have to be fired. But we *will* fire her if we have to, just to be clear."

Yes, it was clear. As was the fact that this whole "powwow" had been arranged for my benefit. There wasn't anything being discussed right now that hadn't already been decided before Dennis and I showed up. No wonder everybody had been taken aback when I started talking about irrelevant things like *blocking*.

Various names were now dropped as possible replacements. Not one was nearly as recognizable as Eve Arden, and we all knew the box office was going to suffer tremendously.

We were going to need a new advertising campaign to promote the new Hedda as well. That plus the extra weeks of theater rental would deeply cut into the postopening advertising budget. The show that was now being referred to around town as the "Eve Arden Show" would have a complete turnaround.

After the initial shock of losing Eve, John and Ricka were convinced that most of the cast would be relieved and that the play would start to work. Or so they told me.

I must admit that I managed a twinge of excitement imagining a Hedda who could actually move and act at the same time, and one who could maybe vary her tempo a little, pick up her cues, say the lines as written—okay, maybe surprise us a little every now and then—and one who could successfully sell the payoff at the finale.

But mostly it all made me horribly sad. Despite our lack of camaraderie, I knew Eve was a nice person, and—no matter what she thought of the play or me—this was really going to hurt her feelings. Her indomitable spirit had kept her going this far. Her return to California would now be so depressing—all because of a lousy play I'd written that her manager and husband had bullied her into doing. It would have been so wonderful had this experience proved to be a triumph—I couldn't think of a living soul who'd wanted anything less for her.

How easy it was to be so charitable toward this irrepressible entity, now that I knew we were about to get rid of her once and for all.

Bret Adams was not invited to Monday night's preview after all. We decided his presence there would have been a surefire alert to Eve that something was up. Joan Copeland, however, was asked to attend, and did so, very discreetly.

The day leading up to this performance was sheer hell. John worked on that infernal last scene, desperately trying to put it into some playable shape.

Damn!" exclaimed Eve after about an hour of this torture. "We never get through this! Not once! We always stop! I'm sorry to be doing this, but I'm just so frustrated!"

"You'll be fine. Let's take it again," said John.

It was a cruel charade for those of us with the knowledge that her days—actually hours—were numbered, and an exercise in painful futility for those who didn't. Nick and June were cardboard figurines throughout the rehearsal. It was obvious to me that these two were close to suicide—or homicide (whichever was quicker).

Curtain time approached at last and I met Brooks backstage.

"Are you going to sit down this evening?" he asked.

"Nope. I'll just be somewhere in the back, as usual." I advised.

"I've actually got a seat tonight." he said. "But it's on the aisle."

The house was not as full as Saturday's. There were barely twenty people upstairs, but the orchestra was full. A few of my friends were there; I smiled but didn't say a word to any of them, retreating to the shadows in the back instead. Andy Matthews saw me coming.

"Oh, no!" he cried. "I'm not standing next to *you!*"

Lights dim, moose bellows, curtain rises. June is flat. Jokes never happen. The pace is deadly, even before Eve's entrance. It is almost as if the audience is aware that they are attending a wake.

After a bad light clue (the malaise is infectious, apparently), Eve makes her entrance. Respects are paid with prolonged applause. From here on, however, it is all downhill. It is Night of the Living Dead *and Eve is our Leading Zombie. She has no idea where she is in the script or much of an idea who she is playing. She hands all the heavy coats to diminutive Gay rather than Stinky. She calls all the characters by a series of random names. She drops lines, adds a few others, and never once is on time for a cue. The rest of the cast continues to act through a fog, with no conviction. One can sense a group cringe spreading through the audience.*

Remarkably, the slapstick in the second act wakes everybody up, and they begin to have what some may mistake as a good time. When Hedda is left on stage to carry the show with Nelson, however, the good humor turns to bile, and a large section of the audience begins to laugh . . . derisively. Funny how you can recognize immediately when they are laughing at you rather than with you.

"The worst is over!" announces Hedda near the final curtain.

This brings down the house. The audience has learned to know better.

Eve's final business is to offer Little Gay—her sole surviving child—the vodka martini the brat has been begging for throughout the entire show. Both the glass she hands her daughter and the one she hands her son-in-law (and recently revealed paramour) are laced with cyanide. So is her own glass, in fact, but at the last minute she is to dump its contents over her shoulder much the same way that Roz Russell disposed of the foul Claude Upson daiquiri several years before in the classic film Auntie Mame. *As the audience sits dumbfounded, with virtually no idea what they are to make of the past two hours of their lives, Eve delivers her final line:*

"Here we have it, then. To you, Gay dearest. My last remaining child. A very special vodka martini…with a twist!"

Instead of artfully tossing her own drink over her shoulder, Eve stands with the glass in tow for several seconds. Finally, as if recalling her business, she ever so slowly tips the glass and lets its contents spill onto the floor in front of her, in full view of her intended victims.

It is the perfect final image for Miss Arden to bequeath to us—a moment of metaphorical incontinence.

The awkward moments continued well after the final curtain descended. Like Laura on the train that is passing through, nobody saw Eve leave. Ricka, John, and I waited in the lobby for Joan Copeland. We had left word with her agent that we would be interested in speaking with her directly after the performance.

We waited.

We waited some more.

Like lost children searching for our mommy, we wandered out onto the street. Miss Copeland was nowhere to be found.

We overheard a woman shrilly addressing a cop passing by:

"Officer! Arrest this show!"

Sure. It's funny *now*.

Dennis and Lillie joined us and the five of us sat glumly in the back of the house to discuss our next move. Or if, in fact, there was even to be a next move.

"We can't afford any more bad word of mouth," warned Ricka. "No more previews. Enough is enough."

We had learned that many of those in attendance Saturday night had been theatrical folk (some of them, naturally, part of June's enormous network of "friends"), and that they were already spreading the word that *Moose Murders* was a bomb. Not just Eve, but the play itself. "Unprofessional" was one of the words of critique that had gotten back to us. "Amateurish" was another. We had no idea that these were to be our most flattering reviews.

As he'd threatened last night at the Dakota, John pronounced that all further previews would be suspended until a replacement was found. And we wouldn't bother calling Joan Copeland's agent. Her absence bespoke volumes.

Eve would be let go first thing in the morning. Bret would be phoned, who would in turn call Glenn to give Eve official notice. The cast would continue to draw full salary. The rental on the O'Neill would continue to be paid.

We all sat in silence for quite some time.

"Knockers up!" said John at last, quoting Snooks.

Home again we went, Dennis and I, and spent quite some time just holding the dog, holding each other, and trying as best we could to keep our heads above water as the steady downpour of despair continued. We fully realized the precariousness of the situation. The budget simply could not withstand any sort of extended suspension of previews. We remembered how long it had taken to negotiate with the other cast members, and here we were looking for somebody to rush into a pivotal role, learn it in a week, and save the play by mid-February. The prospect of closing down completely must be looking awfully good to the producers right now.

The thought of opening the show and being panned by the critics was awful enough. But to have come this far and not to open at all . . . that was simply unacceptable.

Unacceptable.

On top of all this, Dennis and I had both been discerning a growing doubt in Ricka about the show itself. Her allegiance was to John, of course, so we found a little encouragement by his continued conviction that the show *did* work. God knows where he was finding this conviction, but we weren't knocking it.

Another night of sleeplessness at 85 Fourth Avenue.

The news swept through the New York theatrical community at an unbelievable speed. Bret was phoned sometime during midmorning. The gossip columnist Liz Smith (the "Grand Dame of Dish") was first with the story on her Live at Five segment on WNBC. "Something called *Moose Murders*," she reported, "which was to open next Monday, will not—its star, Eve Arden, has dropped out—so who knows what the future of this show will be?"

We returned from dinner to find several messages from Amy Pagnozzi of the *New York Post*: "We understand that Eve Arden has been fired. Please call in reference to this!"

Betty Lee's official press release used the phrase "withdrew amicably due to artistic differences." Eve's departure, it was stressed, was a mutual decision. All concerned began to scramble to save face. Unfortunately, most of us were wholly unprepared to deal with the onslaught of harassment from the press. Ms. Pagnozzi, in particular, was relentless. Along with Dennis and me, she phoned Jerry, June, and Ricka. Betty Lee strongly advised Ricka not to avoid her but to graciously take her call and simply stick to the agreed on talking points in the press release.

The *Post* wanted a story, however, and a better story than a simple explanation of "artistic differences" would provide. There were rampant street rumors. June was convinced that both the *Post* and the *New York Daily News* had planted reporters in the audience Saturday night.

Wednesday's press ran the gamut. The *Times* had a very small article buried in Section C, using the wording of the press release. The *News* ran an article by Patricia O'Haire, using some of the material from an earlier interview with Eve. O'Haire also wrote the following:

"According to rumors around Broadway, the producers are believed to be talking to Polly Bergen, who hasn't been on stage here for quite a while, either, and Elaine Stritch, who has been living in London a number of years."

The article also quoted Eve: "I wasn't as sure about returning here as was my manager—whom I've been with almost as long as I've been with my husband. I had read the script and liked it. I wanted some things changed, but I felt this could be fun. What decided me was when the producers agreed that I could do it for six months only."

But it was Amy Pagnozzi's article in the *Post* that was both the most truthful and the most damaging. "A Star Is Shorn," screamed the headline, "as Producer's Cast Eve from 'Moose.'"

Bad enough, but here's the lead: "Eve Arden, set to make her Broadway comeback after a 42 year absence, has been fired by the producers of 'Moose Murders.'"

> The 70 year-old actress and comedienne was let go when management decided she would jeopardize "Moose Murders'" chances for success.
>
> "It was very difficult to make the decision to let Eve go, but the show would not have survived on Broadway" said producer Ricka Fisher.

"I'm very disappointed. I wish it could have worked out, but it just wasn't right," Miss Arden said last night.

"It was a wild farce, and it was not right for me. We mutually agreed it would be best if I left."

Miss Fisher refused to say whether Miss Arden's age was the factor that caused playwright Arthur Bicknell to make changes in his script, but said the script would be restored to "the way it was originally."

It was this last sentence, along with the verb *fired* that set Bret Adams into a frenzy. He called Ricka and let loose his full agent's wrath, promising legal trouble forthwith. According to Ricka, he was blaming her for the thrust of Amy's article, despite knowing full well this tabloid's loose stance on accuracy when it came to celebrity gossip. John assured the uncustomarily intimidated Ricka that Adams's abuse was being specifically used to gain political leverage—he knew she (Ricka) was a far easier target than the Post itself.

June knew Amy slightly, and told us she was an ambitious *(duh)* twenty-something who knew how to get to the top *(duh, again)*. Amy had told her during their own early-morning phone conversation that Ricka had advised her to call the cast members directly. She was good.

Nasty little rumors about Eve's alleged drinking habits were also circulating now, along with other sordid tidbits about the star's personal habits. Suddenly we were news—and not very pretty news. Force Ten fielded hundreds of calls, and we were all advised to keep our answering machines on.

I made two attempts to contact Eve at the Wyndham, and both times was told there was "no answer" at her room. I suppose I shouldn't have been surprised that she was unwilling or uninterested in speaking to me, since we'd never really "clicked" since those first few torturous hours in Beverly Hills. About the only cast member who'd managed to do so with her—as far as I could tell—was Scott—for whatever reasons. I suspect because he was treating her a lot like Hans Christian Andersen, and reveling in all her fantastic stories. With me, though, Eve had remained distant and impenetrable. One of the most telling signs of her discomfort during this project had been the glazed expression she'd employed throughout most of the rehearsals. She rarely even broke into a smile. I suspected even then that I would always hold at least a little resentment toward her, for never once acknowledging the work I put into the show to cater to all her "ideas." I felt then (and still do, truth be told) that she took all this for granted, as if I'd been employed to render exactly this sort of service.

But this ultimate frosty shoulder really resonated deeply. It hurt like hell. Because I also felt profoundly sorry for this extremely gracious and gentle lady, who had found herself enduring such obvious agony day after day. Not only the chagrin of not being able to cut it on stage, but the burden of steadfastly maintaining a vibrant image for her public. She could never just schlep out of the Wyndham to put in her day's work, she had to spend hours with her makeup and wardrobe, as if she was preparing for a big Hollywood epic. The Eve Arden persona was formidable, and her pride—at least at first—matched it. To see both shattered during those two previews was unspeakably sad.

Although I was never to see or speak to Eve again, the press reported that she would be staying in New York to finish her book. I wondered if *Moose Murders* would be a chapter, or even a mention. More likely, I decided, the play was destined to be permanently stricken from her résumé.

Chapter Eight:

Miss Holland's Opus

Rehearsal was called for eleven on Wednesday morning. Suzanne stood in for Hedda as the search for Eve's replacement continued.

As the News reported, Stuart did contact Elaine Stritch, whose availability was confirmed. She'd recently lost her husband, though, and wanted to return to the theater for "therapeutic" reasons, which did not portend well under these urgent circumstances. We did finally hear from Joan Copeland's agent, who told us what we'd already surmised: Miss Copeland had indeed made a hasty and unannounced exit after Monday's performance, fully convinced that the play didn't work "with or *without* Eve." Anne Francine, likewise, was no longer interested. Peg Murray was also represented by Bret Adams, so we didn't even bother attempting to contact her.

Stuart suggested Jane Powell; he'd directed her in the past and knew her to be a quick study. Ricka called her early in the morning, just as she was going out the door, and made arrangements to have a "serious conversation" later that evening.

While we waited for those negotiations, Stuart began to push Holland Taylor. Her critically acclaimed run in *Breakfast with Les and Bess* had recently ended at the Hudson Guild, and we were told she had experience stepping into projects on short notice. Her manager was sent a script immediately, and, by midafternoon, he had notified Ricka that he "loved it." (Ever notice how many people in this business *love* things? We're all so affectionate.) He was handing it right over to Miss Taylor.

Unfortunately, news of Jane Powell's "involvement" had already leaked out. And the very next morning, The *News* ran another article by Patricia O'Haire with the headline "Will Powell Go Straight?"

"Jane Powell," the article began, "the movie and musical comedy star, 'has been approached' about taking over Eve Arden's role in 'Moose Murders,' the new comedy-mystery."

Within this article, Miss Powell was quoted as saying: "I'd love to do a straight play. But I haven't read the script on this one and I don't know anything about it. I'd love to do a musical, too, if one came along, but I'd prefer a straight play."

We get it, Jane. These days, with billing, you'd consider a *high wire act*; so don't count you out.

Poor Jane (or *fortunate* Jane, whichever way you want to look at it) was contacted that same morning and told that "legal problems" had caused a delay. The producers were sorry for any "misunderstanding." The insouciant star of *Seven Brides for Seven Brothers* was completely amicable.

Hours after this conversation had taken place, the cast members of *Moose Murders* were all phoned individually to be informed that the new Hedda Holloway was to be Holland Taylor.

Nick, I think, was the most elated, since he had been most noticeably affected by Eve's disability on stage.

"I can finally have some fun with that last scene!" he told me outside the theater late that afternoon, as we admired a collage of production shots featuring Eve Arden—all of which, of course, would now have to be replaced, along with all the ads, the marquee, the posters, and the Playbills.

The resulting press regarding Holland's selection made things look pretty damn cheerful, and we could sense a rekindling of public interest. We thought Liz Smith was being a little snippy, though, when she reported in her Thursday column that "Kaye Ballard will host a Sunday luncheon at The Common Good for pal Eve Arden (they starred in *The Mothers-in-Law* together). Eve's children are coming in from California in spite of the fact that mom has dropped out of B'way's *Moose Murders*. Eve is a major talent and somebody should come up with a good play for her in a hurry."

We were all now experts at identifying even the most benign implications, so this and the Dame of Dish's initial referral of "something called *Moose Murders*" made us really defensive. So much so that we went whining about her to Betty Lee.

"Don't worry." Betty Lee assured Ricka. "Liz will do *fine* by you tomorrow!"

And, sure enough, Friday's column included a large photo of Holland and the following blurb:

The show must go on and "Moose Murders" will—in spite of the withdrawal of Eve Arden from the cast this week. The producers picked one of this column's favorite actresses, Holland Taylor, as a replacement. The vivacious comedian is now cramming down 25 pages of dialogue a day and the show will open Feb. 22 at the Eugene O'Neill.

"Moose Murders" is a demanding physical farce with some marvelous actors in it—Lillie Robertson, Nicholas Hormann, June Gable, and now, Holland.

I understand the producers offered Holland her name above the title, probably as a result of her recent Off Broadway work in "Breakfast with Les and Bess." The actress said no, she'd go along with the crowd. "This play demands ensemble performances, it's not a star turn" she is reported to have remarked.

The *New York Post* chimed in:

Miss Taylor says she's stepping into the shoes of an actress who is "one of the great stars of my lifetime, a legend." As for taking over with less two weeks to prepare after Miss Arden was "let go" from the production on Wednesday, the 40-year-old actress told our Diane Stefani: "One blessing is that you don't have time to worry. I have to work close to 24 hours a day. But the cast is lovely, extremely friendly and supportive. I gather they don't dare take the risk in not. We have a situation of urgency."

It was amazing how things perked up once the heavens parted and Holland rode down to the stage in her golden basket. Even June, who had let the lousy attitudes of her ubiquitous theater friends influence her tremendously—friends who had lovingly advised her that she was in a bomb and should seek any escape mode she could while she still had use of her legs—threw us for a loop by chirping after Thursday's first readthrough with Holland: "Hey! She's terrific! I think we have a shot!"

She'd brought in a bottle of champagne for the occasion, and we all gathered in her dressing room to toast our new arrival.

Holland was very aggressive, more than three decades younger than Eve, and gave the role a vitality we hadn't even been able to imagine. She provided a blessed panacea for the cast and for the production itself. The cue pickups began to sizzle and spark, and, before long, we had a full blown, action-packed farce on our hands.

Holland was by no means either warm or fuzzy, but I don't see how those characteristics could have been to anyone's advantage in this situation. She tended not to let me finish my sentences, but when you really got down to it, who had the time to wait for me? We had to get this sucker moving!

By the second runthrough she was completely off book. Her complaints started about that time, too, mostly about the constant drone of the rain.

"It's incredibly distracting," she said. "I can't hear myself think!"

Those of us in the audience were having a hard time hearing her, too. Maybe this was because we finally *wanted* to hear Hedda.

John's directing was put to the test as well, possibly for the first time. Certainly nobody had ever been quite so contentious before. And, remarkably, he started to match her vitality, both physically and vocally. Rather than slumping back in his seat, he was jumping all around the stage, talking to all of us, not just Holland. He started clearing up a lot of the congestion that we'd all long since taken for granted. Some of this was inevitable, since the flaccid directions given to Eve to accommodate her limited mobility all needed to be dropped. At one point Holland suggested that Hedda move across the stage to the fireplace as she spoke one of her lines.

"I don't know," pondered John. "It's an awful long way to the fireplace."

"John," said Holland sternly. "I can move."

Hedda could move. Such a profoundly simple and wonderful truth.

We all needed to seriously readjust our thinking to embrace it.

Scott now had his own special problem as Stinky, of course. His attraction to his mother suddenly made some sense.

"How far should I go?" he asked John.

"I don't know," said John. "But I'll tell you when you get there."

The more active John became, the more his personality began to change, as well—and not always for the better. He was now frequently short-tempered, maybe because he was *just* discovering what hard work directing can be. Personally, I loved this new John—irritability and all. The natives had all been getting a bit restless, including Ricka, and, largely thanks to his efforts, the din of their drums (if not the rain) was getting dimmer.

I cannot say the same for Lillie, who remained rather churlish. She seemed to resent John focusing his attention on anyone other than her—especially Holland. None of us was used to John having a spine or any kind of strong opinion, but Lillie definitely wasn't at all happy with the transformation. John did pay attention to her, often, in fact, and helped her to achieve some very good moments. But as soon as he moved on to somebody else, she'd drop whatever she'd set, and fall back to wherever she'd been before John's guidance. Such was the ballet she chose to perform now. And her diction was deteriorating by the moment, as evidenced by Ricka's new nickname for her: Mush Mouth.

Holland continued to be an inspiration, and her no-nonsense approach to her own business extended to all those around her, as well. There was little or no patience for flubs or missed cues, and the rest of the cast was often jolted by this reversal of roles. Since when did Hedda get to call the shots? What had this farce come to? Even star pupil Mara Hobel unknowingly crossed the line with her new momma, and lived to regret it.

While clinging to Holland during their opening tableau, Mara discovered that she could get quite a few laughs by imitating Holland's facial expressions. The more she carried on, the louder the laughs became, and John did nothing to stop them—or her. This really wasn't anything new; the cast had been operating on a pretty basic *every person for oneself* philosophy of acting since long before Holland's arrival. So it came as a huge surprise to our littlest impressionist when Holland finally rapped her heavy metal ring soundly on the exact center of the young girl's skull. The shock of this assault, of course, superseded any pain at first, so it wasn't until well into the scene that Mara suffered her nervous breakdown and ran screaming and sobbing into the wings of the stage and into the arms of her birth mother.

Without flinching a muscle, Holland watched this backstage activity between Mrs. Hobel and her daughter for a moment, and then turned her head back to us and said resolutely:

"She's young. She'll learn."

And, as I believe I've previously mentioned, Mara was a very quick learner. She never so much as raised an imitating eyebrow ever again.

Holland took me aside with John later that same day to discuss the dreaded final scene and her own personal problems with the transition. At this point I was seriously tempted to suggest substituting a big Hawaiian number involving the entire cast for this fiasco of a scene, but I furrowed my brow in my best Arthur Miller fashion and tried to concentrate on what Holland was saying.

"It's a zany play," she said, "and this idea came to me while I was brushing my teeth this morning. I just don't think it's finished when Hedda says 'with a twist—' we're just not sure what's going to happen to her. So, I thought—what if we see a huge Godzilla-like moose from outside the windows—about to devour the lodge as the curtain falls?"

Here's the thing. I just copied those words from my journal and I'm thinking…what a *great* idea! A big old mechanical moose literally chews up the scenery and we're done with the whole stinking mess! Brilliant! Give that woman a raise! Or better yet, let her out of her contract! She's earned it!

But back then, cramped and exhausted, tired of living and sick of typing, all I could say (apparently) in response to this ingenious deus ex machina was "How funny." I dismissed this whole episode in my journal by claiming that "we simply haven't the time for her suggested improvements to materialize to any great degree."

Don't get me wrong; I'm sure the play still would have flopped, but just think of the fun the critics could have had if they'd soldiered through Holland's proposed second act.

And then the play ate itself.

While we struggled along during this closed rehearsal period, the rest of the theater crowd was understandably beset with curiosity regarding the ill-fated "Eve Arden Show." Jane got a message one day from her agent, Sheldon, and, thinking it was regarding her upcoming American Conservatory Theater auditions, called him back excitedly from a midtown phone booth.

"So!" said Sheldon when he picked up. "What's the scoop with *Moose Murders*?"

I think I may have heard her scream all the way down on Fourth Avenue.

My brother Bruce did his best to cheer me up. He met me for lunch one day to relate some irresistible news. "Your poster at My Great Aunt Fanny's has been desecrated," he announced. "Eve Arden's name has been crossed out, and they blacked out the 'e-r-s' in 'Murders' and put a capital 't' over the 'm.' You know what that *leaves* you with."

"Moose Turds."

"Isn't it awful? Shouldn't your producer march in and tear that poster off the wall?"

"He's kind of busy right now."

"Oh. Well, then, what *does* a producer do?"

Fair enough question, I thought.

Despite hopeful "buzz" like this, the first preview on Friday was a downer. There was a blizzard in Manhattan which closed several other shows . . . which would have worked to our advantage had people not been advised to "stay in their homes." Even the elements were against us, it would seem, as we played to less than half a house and the show fell flat.

Saturday went considerably better. It was a sharp, snarky audience that seemed to get off on the inherent irreverence of the play, and actually enjoyed watching the villains get away with their crimes. Gay's death met with a burst of applause. Take that as you will; *we* became hopeful again.

Monday's performance was quite animated. This was because the actors, all on their own, mind you, decided to do a speedthrough. I think they managed to cut a good twenty minutes off the show, much to the joy of several people involved—including a major portion of the audience, I'm sure. Tuesday went back to a normal pace (John had apparently "noted" them), and yet another tiny audience responded favorably.

Wednesday's matinee was our first senior citizen event, complete with walkers, canes, hearing devices, and the endless drone of clutch purses being snapped open and closed. The show seemed to distract them all sufficiently, but it was at this particular performance that I discerned a lack of real form in the production itself. For maybe the first time, I allowed myself to face the fact that it had been directed by a dilettante.

And this horrible realization stayed with me right through Thursday and Friday's previews, despite the overall improvement of the performances.

Jane, in the audience for the first time on Friday, was understandably obsessed with what she considered to be the "violation of Snooks Keene."

"Snooks is your *Everyman* in the world of *Moose Murders*," she said, "and has very little sense of humor other than her sarcasm. Everything is very serious to her. June's playing her like a slut—that dress is all wrong, by the way—she's like a Loni Anderson with a foul mouth. She's an unsympathetic character who's detracting from the plot rather than helping to put it into focus."

It's only fair to say at this point that my feelings about June Gable's talent had not diminished in the slightest. She appeared to be singularly difficult to control, yes, but I knew others had done it with glowing results. Especially after talking with Jane, I was now throwing most of the blame—if not all of it—on John-not-just-a-dilettante-but-a-fucking-coward Roach. He was helpless, I now understood with the insight of the undead, in the hands of anyone with a will stronger than your average blade of grass. If all of the actors are left to their own devices, doesn't it stand to reason that at least one or two of these devices might not be the *right* devices? And all of the actors, even the ones making incorrect choices—hell, especially the ones making incorrect choices—deserve to be guided in one—count it, one—direction—and to get the leadership that would at the very least put them all in the same play—working toward the same goal.

I mean, this was basic Stanislavski, right?

After the show, Jane and I sent Dennis home with what was gradually turning into a good solid case of walking pneumonia, and headed for Barrymore's . . . until I realized that any theater haunt would not be the place to dish the show the way I *knew* Jane and I were about to dish the show. So we ended up at Marc's, and let loose.

I asked them both if either thought there was any chance that the writing would shine through the messy production.

"No," said Jane. "But I don't think you'll be the only one raked over the coals. After all, there's so much to choose from."

Hardly what I'd call comforting words, despite their dead-on accuracy.

After this candid little powwow, I pretty much sleep-walked my way through the rest of the previews straight on to opening night. To sleep, perchance to dream, you understand. I imagine I gave the impression of being right there at the moment with everybody else, but, trust me, it was all an illusion. I had only a vague awareness of special events like shopping for opening night gifts and being fitted for my first tuxedo. I suspect my mind just gave up and let my body take over this day-to-day living and functioning obligation.

There was tension within the cast. Holland had already demonstrated a tantrum-laced aggressiveness during the first week of working her into the show. Despite my haziness (or perhaps *because* of it), she and I came to task over that damned last scene. She vehemently opposed the language, granting that it would get laughs, but not, she insisted, "appropriate" laughs. As noted, I was sick of this scene, and the last thing I wanted to do was to rewrite it yet again for another damn actor. I hated them all, at this point, the young and the old and the tall.

Our altercation reached screaming levels, I hate to admit. But as Holland and I carried on like Godzilla vs. Rodan, John sank further back into his seat, refusing to take part. Eventually, in disgust, Holland walked to the foot of the stage, cupped her palm over her brow and whined into the darkness: "But, of course, I'll do whatever I'm told to." Which is when

I would have given anything to hear John say "Then do it as *written.*" But nothing. He was invisible.

I left the theater feeling beaten and betrayed. It wasn't so much that John did not support me—he probably did—it's just that his nature didn't allow him to communicate this support out loud. Or, for that matter, to take up the reins and steer this runaway coach to the side of the road. I was deathly sick of the ineptitude, told Dennis as much, who in turn related my feelings to Ricka. Ricka was no moron. She had come to understand the problems as clearly as we did, but, again, what could she do? A vanity production constrains all its participants.

Holland and I made up later in the week. A lot of her anxieties were unavoidable. She had less than two weeks to pull the show together. Truth be told, I really felt that she was one of the few who clearly understood what I was attempting with the script, and her contributions to its structure were immeasurable. No one could do it alone, though, and despite her dead-on approach and searing talent, Holland (in those days, anyway) had one very basic shortcoming. Her technique was bubbly, subtle, and throwaway—something that works like a charm on TV, but kills on stage. You just couldn't hear a word she said.

Now I sincerely believe she *knew* this, despite all her remonstrations to the contrary. She refused to admit that it had anything to do with her vocal equipment or how she was using it. Instead, the culprit became the rain and the thunder loop—an incessant drone that Holland felt was subliminally sabotaging the production. And she had a damned good point, trust me. The rain was so intrusively steady and loud, the cast must have felt at times as if they were doing the nonmusical version of *Two by Two*.

Mind you, John never once said "Holland—speak up! We can't hear you in the fourth row!" Once, and only once, he told her in passing, "You tend to trail off the ends of your sentences," but he gave no emphasis to this note and the problem persisted. Just as he assumed he had given June a clear through line for Snooks, he also assumed he'd harped to Holland about her inaudibility. I think he decided early on that it was his unlucky lot to be working with petulant actors who stubbornly refused to follow his direction. I don't think he ever really knew how very little direction he offered anyone at any time. Perhaps he just overestimated his telepathic powers.

The evening before the Saturday matinee preview, Dennis and I stayed home and listened to the original cast recording of Stephen Sondheim's *Merrily We Roll Along*. Here was a show about ambition, creativity, loyalty, and the rise, fall, and corruption of success in the theater—all enacted by a bunch of people our own age. We didn't have a chance. We both sobbed uncontrollably throughout—first because we identified with the character's mercurial rise to fame and fortune, and later because we became terrified that "Our Time" had come and gone before we'd even been able to enjoy it, let alone abuse it. The score still takes me back to this tumultuous time in my life, and always makes me think of Dennis, Jane, Sally, and Marc—my own "Old Friends" who went through all this turmoil by my side, for better or worse—far, far worse.

The matinee the next afternoon went well (and by now you understand how relative a term I believe "well" to be), but the audience was our worst yet. The few attending were mostly "paper—" folks pulled in off the streets with freebies—and many of them resembled the asylum inmates from a production of *Marat Sade*.

In his own humble way, one of these street folks was about to make arcane Broadway history. I think it's best to let John Simon tell you about him, as he chose to first do in the final paragraph of his *New York Magazine* review published on March 7:

> ...and sitting in front, on the afternoon I attended, were creatures if not from the Black Lagoon, surely from the neighboring gutter. One enormous, pear-shaped individual, arriving late with vomit down his shirt front, smelled so bad that he sent three nearby critics and their companions scurrying for the back of the theater, and, by intermission, had emptied out several rows around them. "Moose Murders" is the only stage play I ever saw in Stereo-odoriferous Smellorama.

Two of those folks Simon watched flee to the back of the theater turned out to be Frank Rich and his companion for the afternoon, Wendy Wasserstein. Rich has talked about this inauspicious introduction to the play often enough that I now feel I was there suffering along with him—even though my journal tells me I was not. John opted not to tell any of us (including the cast) that this particular matinee was to be seen not just by Rich and Simon, but by Doug Watt of the *News* and Clive Barnes of the *Post* as well. Had I known all the gods from Critics Valhalla would be descending to earth to convene at the O'Neill on that particular afternoon, I certainly would have been right there front and center with our vomit-covered, pear-shaped, papered patron.

Blissfully unaware that we were already stinking up the place and emptying the theater of all but the most stalwart or feeble-minded, we completed the two previews on Saturday and felt pretty good about ourselves. I got a call from June on Sunday morning, who'd just spoken to a number of her friends who'd seen the show.

"They tell me there's a much better play here than I'm doing," she revealed, and began to talk about that "conservative and vulnerable" center to Snooks that had been essentially absent since day one. Since by now I knew the critics had already made their decisions about the play, I found June's epiphany a tad *moot*, but this didn't stop me from immediately phoning John with the news.

"June now knows who she is." I said. "She's figured out her character with the help of all her theater friends."

There was a long pause.

"I hate that woman," John said.

Chapter Nine:

An Open and Shut Case

"I thought I'd come here and do nothing but gush," said our friend Alan Heppel at dinner Monday night. He'd flown in from LA the day before to join us for the opening and had just gotten his feet wet by sitting through the last preview with us. "But you're both so objective and in control, I guess I can speak frankly."

Who the hell had given him *that* idea? Still, it was good to have my old buddy from high school there with me, and it would be equally good for Dennis to have Brother Aelred on hand, too. The Mad Monk was due to fly in from Seattle the next day. Maybe we'd find our strength in larger numbers—or at least some kind of shield from the slings and arrows we were about to suffer.

"We have the support of the church and the civil authorities," Dennis said. "Now all we need is a doctor."

But instead we got Dennis's mother, Mary Ann, who also arrived Sunday. She was in the way, and fairly aware of it, but banking on receiving the customary civility from her son and me—his special friend. She wasn't at all prepared for the negativism we were both spewing. The intended success of *Moose Murders* was going to change her life, she had decided, and this vested interest was being abused and shattered in front of her eyes. She couldn't understand why we weren't happier, or why we were so seldom willing even to *talk* to her about the upcoming event. She busied herself inventing errands to run and trying to be helpful, but we were quite beyond help at this point.

Brother Aelred arrived early Tuesday morning. After picking him up at JFK and then dropping him off at his hotel, Dennis and I made arrangements with a florist to deliver single roses to everybody in the cast, and then sped off to Macy's to finish our opening night shopping.

Dennis picked up our tuxedos as I hurriedly wrapped fourteen gifts—all the while listening to afternoon soap operas blare out from the TV—Mary Ann's constant stimulant.

She liked them loud. I was trying to make peace with my God. We were not good company for each other.

The rented limousine arrived at five. Mary Ann snapped a couple of pictures of her son and his very close friend in our tuxes, and argued with Dennis on the way downstairs about taking more pictures of the limo. "Later," mumbled Dennis.

We picked up Brother Aelred at the hotel and began the somber pilgrimage to the theater. As Dennis and I pensively peered through the smoked glass windows, Aelred finally broke the silence. "The similarity between this ride and a funeral procession is unmistakable," he said. Mary Ann punched him reproachfully on the arm and looked to the two of us to refute the comment. We didn't, and we all rode on without much additional conversation.

When we reached the O'Neill, Aelred mercifully escorted Mary Ann to a bar while the two of us snuck in through the stage door and distributed our gifts. On our way to each dressing room, we stumbled over dozens of floral arrangements, packages, bottles of champagne, and glittering banners. Lillie's dressing room alone was stuffed with so many floral wreaths and long-stemmed roses it must have been hard for her to find enough room to greasepaint her face. There were countless telegrams waiting for us from Ithaca College, and our friends from all walks of our lives. There was an especially ornate card from the Shubert Organization.

Joe Allen had sent bouquets to everyone, too—no doubt to welcome our inevitable inclusion into his rogues' gallery.

We opened up as many gifts along the way as we deposited: a pair of crystal Tiffany liqueur glasses from Holland, hand-decorated egg shells commemorating the event, from Jack, and an exquisite set of Hoffritz cutlery from John and Lillie, with ivory-carved moose on each handle.

Knives. All sizes. The most expensive ones you could own. An extra fancy set of moose memorabilia or an extra fancy subliminal message? No time to decode now; must move on, move on.

Dennis left to retrieve his mother and Aelred, and I waded through the carnations and chrysanthemums to throw myself at the mercy of the friends and family members that had begun to accumulate. It was a crazy kaleidoscope of faces from all my years on earth. I half expected Howard

Morris as "Uncle Goopy" from the old Sid Caesar parody of *This Is Your Life* to burst out of the crowd and wrap himself around my leg. Jane was there with her mother, proffering more gifts that would have to wait to be opened until the party at Sardi's after the show. Marc had squeezed himself into a ten-year-old suit and was concerned about where he'd be sitting this evening. I worked my way through kisses and hugs and more gifts, into the bar where Brother Aelred and Mary Ann were just finishing their cocktails. It was here that I confronted my oldest brother Harrison, his wife Jane, and their youngest son, my nephew Bruce.

You have to understand something. We Bicknells are not big on reunions, especially when the occasion calls for joy. So, for the first few hours, at least, this was a horribly awkward time for all of us.

Harrison, it turned out, was in a bit of a panic. All the Bicknell tickets had been picked up by our other brother Bruce the day before—and Bruce, apparently, was somewhere between LaGuardia and the O'Neill with our Uncle Arthur and Aunt Emma in tow.

"There's a holdup in the Bronx, Brooklyn's broken out in fights . . ."

I listened as best I could about how difficult the traffic was in this city and how outrageously steep the rates were at the New York Hilton (where Uncle Arthur was staying) until the lights began to flash and the crowd began to file inside.

I remained outside with Harrison scanning faces for Bruce, grateful for such a specific task. Bruce and party finally appeared, and before I knew what was happening, I was having my picture taken by an irrepressible Aunt Emma, who was one person having the absolute time of her life. (She was only a Bicknell by recent marriage.)

This may not be the fairest appraisal of what was going on with my family during all this. Most of them had no idea what we'd been living through these past several weeks, and for all they knew the curtain was about to rise on another "Death Trap" or "Sleuth"—had they been able to name a couple examples of successful Broadway mysteries. For better or worse, these were our very last moments to enjoy any sort of hopeful expectation, and we did the best we could with whatever little we had. Even the usually somber Uncle Arthur was flashing a smile as bright as any matinee idol, while Aunt Emma flitted about snapping candid shots like Annie Leibovitz.

We'd managed to comp Jane, her mother, Marc, and Mary Ann. The other two tickets from our party—Brother Aelred's and my own—had been paid for, so I decided to actually use mine and sit with the others in the midsection of the orchestra. I walked in with Rex Reed and tried my best not to look like I was aware of it. I left him somewhere center orchestra, and then went down the aisle a few more rows to take the seat Marc had thoughtfully saved for me. I settled down with him securely on one side and Jane and her mother on the other, and comfortably waited for the thunder clap, the plaintive moose bellow, and the (unbeknownst to some of us, at least) swan song performance of Snooks and Howie's "Jeepers Creepers."

It might have been where I was sitting, but the show's reception seemed very good. Granted, the seats were filled with family and friends but, I've got to say, neither group was particularly known for exhibiting any wayward, overzealous display of tolerance. I was even able to mingle and receive compliments at intermission, something I'd assiduously avoided since wandering downstairs to use the restroom during one of the previews, and being gut-kicked by bits and pieces of overheard "critiques." The only thing that had saved me then had been my anonymity and the good sense I had to make a hasty exit. Tonight, conversely, I was wearing a lapel pin a friend had made me of the terrified Moose logo with a thought bubble over its head that read: 'Opening night…' so there might as well have been a red neon arrow pointing at me and following me around.

John, Suzanne, Ricka, and Albert had all chosen not to sit and were clustered together in the back. I saw them all very briefly, and they seemed as encouraged as the rest of us. On reflection, I have to say I'm glad I watched this last show from the house. It was good to be engulfed by the steady flow of giggles and guffaws and even the occasional ooohs or aaahs. For one brief shining moment, this was the opening night of my dreams.

After curtain calls, I sent Brother Aelred and Mary Ann back to the limo, told Jane I'd meet her at Sardi's, and ran backstage to make the climb up to Dennis's dressing room. Such commotion! Countless flowers had yet to be claimed; I tried my best to find any that were ours, but was hurried out the door and into the limo by Dennis, himself full of uncustomary mirth. Something nontoxic was in the air at the moment; God only knows where it had come from, or how long it would last.

The Eugenia Room at Sardi's was elegant and radiant. A dance band was already playing as we checked our coats. Alan met us in what appeared to be a reception line. "I'm on the groom's side," he quipped. He also came up with what was to my mind the best analogy for the evening: "Being at a friend's opening night is like going to Disneyland and studying for your final exams all at once!"

The party was downright festive, with very little foreshadowing of the total decimation only hours away. I do remember Robert Johanson, who'd directed *Masterpieces*, looking at me rather sadly, I thought, and saying to me "Well, Arthur—you've written a funny play."

Oh, oh. There's that word "funny" standing alone in the cold wind again, without its overcoat or scarf.

Harrison took me aside and said "I can't say I understood everything I saw and heard…but if the reviews are bad, I'll have to disagree with them."

"But," he added before returning to his table, "I won't be able to agree with the *good* ones, either."

That should cover everything; I understood.

The food was yummy, or so I was told. I preferred to drink. And the drinks were endless. Everywhere I looked there were friends and family from all over the country, basking in the glow of Arthur and Dennis's Broadway Debut. I'd brought the Polaroid, and like the documenting fool I am, made sure I'd gotten a portrait of just about everybody present. It was worth it, of course, both now and then. These wonderful people—all of them—with their devotion and untarnished affection—made up a force field that was absolutely overwhelming—and was later to provide a desperately needed sanctuary.

Around eleven, the crowd quickly and methodically began to thin. Most of them knew what was coming, and that it would be safest not to be around when the tsunami actually hit the beach. Ricka and Dennis left for the publicist's office, both of them forbidding me to tag along. This gave me an extra forty-five minutes of blissful ignorance.

The band, without warning, began to play "Nearer My God to Thee."

No, not really, but wouldn't that have been ballsy?

Harrison gathered up brother Bruce, Uncle Arthur, and the rest of his clan. He jotted down my phone number so he could call "first thing in the morning." What either one of us would find to talk about then was beyond our imagination, I'm certain, but it seemed to both of us like a very good way to end things.

Dennis finally returned and drew me away from the others. I remember how gently—how lovingly—he placed his hand on my shoulder and whispered into my ear.

"The *worst*," he said.

Every television critic with the exception of Pia Lindstrom (who was merely ambiguous) went after the show with an almost unprecedented malice. I say "almost," only because my research has not been inexhaustible, and there *might* be a show in the dark ages that gathered equally bad or worse press.

Doubt it, though.

"Atrocious.""Horrendous.""Somebody by the name of Arthur Bicknell . . . who should change his name immediately . . ."

Most of the network commentators mercifully left out names. Many remarked that Eve Arden was fortunate to have abandoned the sinking ship at the eleventh hour. The director and/or his direction were rarely mentioned—the only perpetrator to be singled out besides me was Ricka on behalf of Force Ten Productions.

The dailies were no better. Clive Barnes decided he wouldn't waste people's time with a review. Instead, the *Post* ran a graffiti moose along with the announcement that there would be no review of this inane production. This was perhaps both the cruelest and the kindest decision made by a press member.

I asked Dennis what it had been like in the press room.

"Ricka and I just sat there," he said. "It was one stab wound after another, with no relief. We were glad that you and John weren't there for the massacre."

After a respectful duration, we were quietly joined by John, Lillie, and Ricka. The only cast member still around was Lisa, who now deferentially approached our huddled mass of show refugees.

"Hey, you. Mr. Brilliance," she said in her deep, gravelly voice. "You're before your time."

That helped a little, I think. It's hard to separate all the different feelings I was bombarded with at that moment. I know I was truly experiencing them all, though—my body hadn't gone into shock, and I wasn't numb. I was feeling everything very acutely.

I remember Jane approaching me, her eyes wide and sharply focused. "Where do you want me?" she asked. "I'll stay with you—go away—whatever you want."

I didn't actually break down into tears until Jane's mother Mary put her arms around me, stroked the back of my head, and murmured "I love you." My own mommy had been dead for seventeen years, so I'd forgotten how good this kind of maternal hug could be—especially when your heart was breaking.

A small band of us ended up at Curtain Up, a theater restaurant near Manhattan Plaza. We drank, theorized, schemed, drank, commiserated, analyzed, drank, drank, and drank again, well into the morning. After that, Dennis and I saw our out-of-town visitors off, and then stumbled into an all-night diner to discuss the next steps. I believe we had a couple of ideas for next steps, but sleeping definitely wasn't one of them.

The next day Lillie invited us to lunch at a French restaurant on 61st street. This, along with the company of Brother Aelred and, yes, even Mary Ann, provided us with the welcome distraction to help us cope with this especially gloomy day after.

It was raining, of course.

We went back to the O'Neill one last time to pick up some remaining flowers and to say our goodbyes to several cast members. Workers were already depositing large chunks of Marj Kellogg's beautiful set onto the street for trash pickup. This was the single most devastating sight I took in during the whole catastrophe, and I still dream about it sometimes.

"Like a phoenix!" exclaimed Jack, as we walked into the theater.

"Hey!" shouted Holland, when she caught sight of me. "You were killed!"

You bet," I said, as I watched June Gable make her rounds tossing snapdragons into each dressing room.

"Flores. Flores para los muertos! Flores para los muertos!" she chanted.

"Listen," continued Holland. "They wanted this *out*. They were after blood!"

She thought this explained—at least in part—why none of the critics had addressed the play itself in their reviews, other than listing the cast of insufferably inane characters they'd had to endure for two hours.

"They didn't want anyone to misconstrue anything as a possible compliment," she said. "Nothing you could possibly excerpt for an ad to keep the thing running!"

"We're not defeated," I lied.

"Of course not! You're professionals now," she lied back.

But the words made me feel good, I have to admit. If nothing else, I'd paid some dues. Maybe I could take pride in that.

"Flores! Flores para los muertos!"

Then again, maybe not.

June threw me a snapdragon, and then disappeared up the stairwell. I handed the flower to Lillie, who happened to be standing next to me.

"I don't think you got enough of these," I said.

The Lady Roach curtsied sweetly, and accepted her floral scepter.

"You know," she said, "whatever else they can say, we got there!"

True enough, I suppose, but that didn't stop me from recalling a famous quote from Gertrude Stein:

"There is no *there* there."

A week later, *Newsweek* published an article in its business section entitled "A Bad Case of Broadway Blues," which used *Moose Murders* as a major example of a disastrous season so far for 1983. "The bouncy tune of 'The Lullaby of Broadway' has turned into a discordant funeral dirge this year," wrote David Pauly. "Twenty of the 31 shows that opened this season have already closed. Twelve of Broadway's 38 theaters are dark and the ominous shadow will spread in the coming weeks when at least three more shows are likely to close. The venerable Shubert Organization, even with house-fillers like the sizzling new 'Cats' and the long-running 'Dreamgirls,' expects to suffer a 4 percent drop in ticket sales for the season. Says Shubert president Bernard Jacobs, 'Broadway is in a recession, a cyclical slump.'"

My old pal Leo Shull printed a lively little feature in his March 7 edition of *Show Business*, which he labeled "'Moose Murders' is murdered—Investors Are, Too." In it, he offered the information many folks were clamoring for . . . exactly how much fucking money had been dumped into this bad boy. According to Leo (and I have no real way of verifying this—or, let me be more honest, I have no desire whatsoever to fact check this particular issue) Force Ten Productions, Inc. pitched in $376,000 plus another $112,000 from Corbin Robertson (Lillie's brother), and the General Partners (all from Houston) put in $112,000 for a total investment of $600,000.

Just a drop in the bucket by today's standards, of course, but practically unheard of in those days.

And all of it straight down the *terlet*.

So maybe it was all just the sluggish economy that was to blame for Moose Murders' cataclysmic failure. After all, not *everybody* had hated it. Pia Lindstrom had been too confused to offer an opinion, and here's what our friend Liz Smith wrote in the *Daily News* a few days after the closing:

"Say what you will, I feel honored to be one of the elitists who saw 'Moose Murders.' What's more, I had a very good time at the opening night of this farce. It received just about the worst reviews in theater history. Well, as far as I was concerned it wasn't boring for a minute and that's more than I can say for half of the elevated plays I've seen this season."

These were the *only* kind words about the show I saw in print. And, as I mentioned way back at the beginning of this tale, the play stuck in the critics' cumulative craw for weeks after its demise. "The only good thing about 'Goodnight, Grandpa' wrote Michael Feingold of the *Village Voice*, "is that it was better in both execution and intention than 'Moose Murders.'" (I always wondered how Feingold had found out about my "intentions." Perhaps they'd slipped out at the party at Sardi's, which he attended as a guest of two of my friends. Jane had run into him in the buffet line, and, without identifying herself, asked if he'd spoken to our mutual acquaintances about the show. "To tell you the truth, I've been consciously avoiding them" she reported him as saying. "They're friends with the playwright.")

Arthur Bell, also of the *Voice*, complained about Frank Rich's dismissal of '*On Your Toes*,' by suggesting the critic "must have eaten a rancid portion of the 'Moose Murders' set before seeing the show." William Raidy of the *Star Ledger* assured his readers that top Broadway producers promised "a light at the end of the tunnel despite the proliferation of 'trash plays' such as 'Moose Murders.'" (This, from the same man who, in reference to *My Great Dead Sister*, had written about me three years earlier: "The author has eloquence in dealing with his decidedly off-beat characters that reminds me somewhat of Carson McCullers (mixed with today's Albert Innaurato's sense of 'family')." I suspect he never made the connection. Maybe if I'd called this latest opus *The Moose Is a Lonely Hunter*, or something…

So, what's your genre, there, Arthur?

Trash. Trash Plays. Thanks for asking.

A week or so after closing, we visited the Dakota to pick up some stained glass sculptures with the Moose logo a local artist had created for us. John and Ricka seemed a bit shell-shocked, but were both plugging along. Ricka had learned from the press office that the New York City Theatre Criticism Trifecta (Rich, Barnes, and Watt) had allegedly conferred with one another before their reviews were published. They'd all hated Anthony

Shaffer's *Whodunnit,* a play that had opened in December and was still running despite some very mixed reviews. True to Holland's suspicions, perhaps they were convinced that a large factor contributing to the extended run of this "putative comic thriller" had been the producers' use of excerpted quotes that had been annoyingly misconstrued by the public as complimentary. "Stuck in a no-win situation," Rich had originally written, "the good actors trapped in this room generally acquit themselves as honorably as possible."

This statement had been honed to something like "good actors!" for the show's advertising campaign.

The triumvirate apparently wanted to make sure the same advantage would not be available to the producers of *Moose Murders.*

We suggested getting together for a post mortem dinner, but John had already booked himself and Lillie on the next morning's Concorde for a quick restorative jaunt to Paris.

Such are the postdisaster compensatory options for the very rich.

If only he'd waited a month or so, I might very well have been the poor schmuck booking his flight. Crawling back to Air France to resume my day job was one of my own best options, and I gladly took it.

If I were writing the screenplay of these misadventures, I'd end it here, with a panoramic shot of me in a trench coat waving a tearless goodbye from the gate as John and Lillie disappear into the fog at Mach 2.

My last visit to the Dakota came a few weeks later, when I handed in a screenplay John had commissioned me to write. I always suspected this was a bit of a charitable gesture on his part, but considering everything else I'd been forced to swallow these past several weeks, it was easy enough to throw a good chunk of my pride into the stew. And I had rent to pay. I'd get over it.

All traces of the Moose had been removed from his office by then. In their places were posters of two subsequent Broadway projects, both of which had been taken on in the nick of time before the deadline for the 1983 Tony Awards.

The first, a drama starring Richard Dreyfus called *Total Abandon* that dealt with the rape of a small child—always an audience magnet—was received almost as miserably as had been *Moose Murders*—and, like its predecessor, closed after just one performance.

The second, Peter Nichol's *Passion,* garnered mixed reviews and raves for its star Frank Langella and managed to stay open, thereby escaping the one-night-only curse. It opened right under the wire—before the cutoff day for the Tonys—and captured a nomination for its supporting actress, Roxanne Hart.

I'd be lying if I claimed that Dennis and I felt no resentment as John struggled to buy back his name. Both *Total Abandon* and *Passion* listed "John Roach" as a contributing producer, not Force Ten. If only it had been as easy for the two of us to find public absolution. Well. I say that now but the truth is I don't believe I was feeling as devastated as I probably should have been. I don't know if you ever really dare to indulge yourself in either the fantasy of total success or total failure during such theatrical joy rides. Neither one of those extreme situations is real; most outcomes fall into the murky gray middle ground. I can't be sure, but I suspect Abject Failure was as surreal to me as Overnight Success must have been to some of my fellow playwrights, all of whom—at least in *this* narrative—will remain nameless.

In April, just before the Tony awards, Frank Rich wrote an article in the *Sunday Times* about "classic flops." My dead baby was his focal point. Of all the programs he'd collected from the past decade, he claimed, he'd keep only the one from *Moose Murders*. He went on to suggest how much fun it would be in ten years to see how all those involved with the project had gotten on with their lives.

Both Holland and Nick went straight back to the plays they'd left, to take on the Moose—Holland to Off-Broadway's *Breakfast with Les and Bess* and Nick to *The Dining Room*—which ended up playing until mid-July. We took in the show around this time and had a reunion lunch with Nick. For whatever reasons, this was the first time we were really able to get to know one another. I guess we were old war buddies, now. We talked a bit about another upcoming *Moose Murders* mention—this time in the form of a fourteen-page article for *Esquire* written by our own June Gable. It was scheduled, Nick had learned, for the magazine's September issue. He said June had phoned him to forewarn him and to assure him that he himself wouldn't be trashed.

I had to ask who *would* be trashed, of course.

"She zaps it to Ricka and John," revealed Nick. "She refers to me as a 'victim,' calls Lisa 'the tall one,' and apparently comes out smelling like a rose herself."

That was quite an understatement I learned sometime in August when I picked up my own copy of "How I Survived Moose Murders, the

Biggest Broadway Bomb," by June Gable. According to June's revisionist theories, John and Ricka had clearly bound and gagged "Love Lump" (a term of endearment June claimed her agent used on her when presenting her with good news—like being cast as the Old Lady in *Candide* and being offered a lead in *Moose Murders*) and forced her to do these unnatural acts on a public stage against her will. Despite this mental and physical abuse (again according to her article), she'd remained the sweetheart of the set, feeding E.T. lollypops to the little girl to dry her tears, and helping the old lady through her bouts of paranoid dementia. "I turned toward Eve," wrote June, "who looked utterly exhausted. She barely made it out for bows. I touched her cheek, but she just stared straight ahead. I knew I'd never see her in *Moose Murders* again."

Marc and I read this together, giggling like school girls. "I turned toward Eve," we interpolated. "I touched her cheek, drew her impossibly close, and kissed her dry, blistered, open lips, exploring her wisecracking mouth with my barbed and hungry tongue. But she just stared straight ahead.

"'Line?' she gasped, then died in my arms."

Listen, I think June was smart to grab a buck where she could. I myself never quite found a way to capitalize on any of this crap. I *was* approached by somebody claiming to represent both Sandra Bernhard and Paul "Pee Wee Herman" Reubens. Seems these two were interested in teaming up to coproduce a musical version of *Moose Murders*. Like everybody else, they'd been intrigued by the unbelievably lousy reviews. Their whole concept, in fact, seemed to hinge on a collection of gigantic billboards with excerpts from all of the most quotably egregious critical beratement (John Simon's "as close as I ever have to get to the bottomless pit," for example). They even had a working title: *Moose Murders, the Afterbirth*.

But I turned them down. Probably a stupid move on my part, but I just wasn't into the whole cult thing; I was still seeing myself as a serious *playwright of promise*.

Liz Smith tried to help me gather some postproduction momentum. She wrote another column suggesting that some smart producer should capitalize on the thousands of people kicking themselves for not attending *Moose Murders*.

Guess all the smart producers out there missed this advice.

The only inquiry regarding foreign rights to the play came from an agency in Istanbul.

That's right. Turkey—and *only* Turkey—wanted the rights to my show. Does it get any better than that?

In 1994, eleven years after the curtain came down on the first and last performance of *Moose Murders*, Frank Rich, leaving his position as chief theater critic of the *New York Times* to become an op-ed columnist, wrote a retrospective essay for the *Sunday Magazine* about his thirteen-year stint as "the Butcher of Broadway." Along with his reminiscences of great plays the likes of *Angels in America, Noises Off,* and the *Heidi Chronicles,* came this:

> Broadway was not all "Amadeus" and "Dreamgirls." At a time when production costs were still low enough for first-time producers to indulge their most catastrophic theatrical whims, covering the theater was as madcap as going to the circus. It became a running gag with me and Wendy Wasserstein, who would accompany me to anything, that many of the biggest bombs on Broadway had titles beginning with the letter M . . . .
>
> "Moose Murders" was a special case. It is the worst play I've ever seen on a Broadway stage. A murder mystery set in a hunting lodge in the Adirondacks, it reached its climax when a mummified quadriplegic abruptly bolted out of his wheelchair to kick an intruder, dressed in a moose costume, in the groin.
>
> Wendy and I saw "Moose Murders" at a Wednesday matinee. Hardly had the play started when the smell of vomit wafted through the orchestra at the Eugene O'Neill Theatre. Gradually, those seated in the first few rows starting taking refuge in empty seats at the back of the house, until finally we and the apparent source of the exodus, a voluminous man third-row center, were virtually the only members of the audience in the front rows. Yet I feared that if we moved back, I might be too far away to give the play a fair shake.
>
> Finally, my sense of justice gave way. I bolted to the back of the theater, where the press agent and other staff members of the production inevitably hang out at critics' performances, to seek a solution. To my amazement, however, there was no one in the back of the house; this sinking ship had already been abandoned. I retrieved Wendy, and we moved to the back row, where we watched the unfolding horror with no less amazement than we had from close up. "Moose Murders" closed on opening night, but its gallant cast members still list the credit in their Playbill biographies, usually preceded by the word "legendary." (Frank Rich. "After 13 years of drama and farce. . . EXIT THE CRITIC. . . humming the music and settling the scores." *New York Times Magazine.* February 13, 1994.)

For years I was one of those "gallant" folks opting to use the word *legendary* whenever talking about that particular life-defining production.

I wrote other plays, enjoyed a few productions of one or two of them here and there—none ever again on the scale of on or Off Broadway. Eventually I left Air France to start a career as a literary agent, and, a few exciting and harrowing years after that, found myself unable to cope with the stress and expense of living in New York City one second longer, and ultimately escaped to—of all places—Springfield, Massachusetts. I went there to live with Dennis (with whom I reunited after an estrangement of over a decade) and a litter of golden retriever puppies. That fantasy I talked about in the prologue about writing a great redemptive play never happened, but I did land a decent job as receptionist and—just a few patiently humble months later—communications director for the city's regional theater, StageWest. A year or so after the theater went under (as so many do, sadly), I found shelter in Springfield's *other* bastion of culture, Merriam-Webster, the reference publisher, and stayed there as the company's publicist for eleven years—longer than I'd worked at any day job in my life.

Perhaps not the most exciting existence, working with the lexicographers and "harmless drudges" (as Noah Webster himself once put it), but happy enough—certainly safe and remote enough to allow me the luxury of almost completely forgetting about that bitch from the preview audience so many years ago who'd screamed "Officer! Arrest this play!" about something that had taken me at *least* an entire month to write.

The first shoe had fallen so miserably, why on earth should I continue to wait for the other one? Time to bury the Moose, and to inter the good and bad with its bones.

And then, wouldn't you know it, those damned *Moose Murders* journals that I'd suspiciously left behind in the early 90s somewhere inside my Upper West Side sublet were anonymously delivered to my friend Sally's work address in Manhattan. Only a few weeks after that, Sally actually remembered she *had* them, and hurriedly sent them off to me in Massachusetts.

Around that time Dennis was diagnosed with a brutally aggressive brand of prostate cancer, and I began a race to finish this book before he left us. Unhappily, we lost both the race and Dennis in February of 2008. But the home hospice nurse had taught me that the sense of hearing is one of the last things to go, so those final days were made almost bearable by bedside readings of our old misadventures, his and mine.

Dennis's horrible and slow death put a stop to my writing for a very long time. It seemed that I was not meant to gain even a sense of closure on this Moose issue.

And then—just like that unexpected run-in with your intended soul mate that they always say will really and truly happen one day if you just stop looking for it—almost *exactly* like that but maybe a little more *unexpectedly*—I got a phone call from self-described "part-time conceptual artist," John W. Borek.

"Arthur," said Borek, "I've ruined your play."

He had me at *ruined*.

Who Is John Borek?

Racing through the past quarter-century of my life post Moose Murders in a few paragraphs creeps me out a little, especially when I see that I've chosen to devote only a few scant sentences to Dennis's bout with cancer. I'm not trying to be cavalier about that awful period of my personal history, or in any way attempting to marginalize the experience. It was an excruciatingly sad, joyless time. His death process from start to finish was just about as long as the play's entire life span from paper to production, and was— despite not being reviewed by the press—significantly more painful to endure. I began writing this memoir before he got really sick, and fully anticipated his still being around when I finished. It's now been three years since his death, and the damn book still isn't done. I guess what I'm feeling now as I struggle to conclude this story is a big fat case of survivor's guilt, on more than one level.

F. Scott Fitzgerald said *there are no second acts in American lives*. If I buy that, and I'm not sure I *don't*, it just presents another impediment to finishing this off. See, this story is about *Moose Murders*, which is infamous, and not about Arthur Bicknell, who is not. Certainly within the traditional restraints of a memoir, having at any time during one's life created some-thing considered to be "the golden standard of awfulness against which all theatre is judged" is an extremely difficult act to follow with any kind of epilogue. Anything you talk about—even nonmetaphorical death—is bound to be at least a little anticlimactic.

More inanely put, in order to even *pretend* to destroy this monstrous master flop of mine once and for all, I needed a better stake to drive straight into its dead little heart.

A nice healthy slew of amateur productions throughout the years might very well have given me the button I was seeking, but the truth is, there haven't been very many of these at all.

Bad play, you know.

I was guest-of-honor at one extravaganza, though, performed in Lancaster, Pennsylvania, where blind Howie was played by a local Mennonite and where the whole production was treated like an old-fashioned melodrama, and where the audience was encouraged to boo for the villains and cheer for the heroes. I was very interested to see which characters the director had chosen to be the heroes—probably because I'd never been able to figure that one out for myself.

Attention was almost exclusively reserved for the big bull moose head mounted on the back wall of the set for another production, this time in Skowhegan, Maine. The hairy trophy was reportedly a recent kill made especially for the show by one of the theater's most devoted patrons. The dead moose got its own bio in the program, and I discovered its body as an entree choice at the adjacent restaurant—along with a nice chocolate mousse for dessert. (I tried neither, as I recall.)

The other thing I remember about this production was that little Gay was played by a thirty-year-old woman who might also have played Josie in *A Moon for the Misbegotten*. She never unbuckled her tap shoes, and trod mighty heavily on those boards for the entire show—whether she happened to find herself on or off the stage. Visually, this show was about fresh moose meat. Otherwise, it was all about Gay's shoes.

By far the most Poetically Just revival happened in 2007, when a repertory company in the Philippines opened their fortieth year of continuous productions with "Moose Murders by *Frank Rich*." Although I didn't make the trip to see this particular rendition, I Googled like mad, and, sure enough, Frank's name was listed as author on all the company's press material. "This mystery farce by Frank Rich," read one release, "has been dubbed by its director an outrageous comedy that was written ahead of its time." More than a year later they corrected their error and wrote a sort of retraction ("it was a guy named Arthur Bicknell"), but had they chosen not to bother, I'm going to come clean right now and admit that their horrible little secret would have been safe with me forever.

Sometime in the spring of 2008 my old friend Karen Winer got in touch with me at Merriam-Webster. She told me I had to register with that new social networking phenomenon called Facebook in order to be able to see some fabulous photographs of a staged reading of *Moose Murders* her equally old and dear friend John was organizing in Rochester. I fought off signing up as long as I could (probably a matter of hours), logged on, saw the photos, and soon became hopelessly dependent on Facebook and all the connections—real and otherwise—it suddenly afforded me access to.

But that's another story of obsession; back to Borek.

An erstwhile book store owner and current aide to a Rochester city councilman, John W. Borek had just begun to find his niche as a gadabout conceptual artist when our paths crossed. For some time he'd been fascinated with the concept of failure as an art form, and had been searching for just the right discipline in which to express his unorthodox philosophy on the subject. It was his goal to find an example of some such art form—painting, film, music, whatever—universally considered to be the "worst" of its kind, and then to showcase it and its perceived awfulness as a legitimate piece of art.

Pick a category and try this game at home.

It's not so easy, is it? Coming up with *the* worst. Unless, of course, you pick the category of *stage*, in which case the answer is almost always going to be…

Aha!

Yes, once again my poor, tattered, berated little farce was going to be used as a bad example.

"I owe my career to Arthur Bicknell, the most generous playwright of the twenty-first century," claims Borek in the *manifesto* of what he calls his Post-Cap Movement.

"When art becomes business," he explains,

its value is only a matter of success or failure. The creative process exists to please a hierarchy of interests rather than to take on important and controversial matters directly. And, perhaps most importantly, the artist repeats past successes rather than exploring new ideas because the lure of commercial success is so strong.

I founded the Post-Cap Movement in October, 2008 with Post-Cap muse Karen Winer in the midst of presenting a revival of Arthur Bicknell's play *Moose Murders*. The production revisited the worst-reviewed play in Broadway history, a play that effectively put Mr. Bicknell on hiatus as an artist for a quarter century. Two years prior to the Broadway production of *Moose Murders*, Mr. Bicknell had presented a play, *My Great Dead Sister*, that was regarded as one of the best off-Broadway plays of 1981. His abrupt fall from grace and descent into no-artist's land because of one failed play inspired Post-Cap's examination of failure in the arts. Karen and I concluded that the demands of the marketplace and the expectations of returns on investment in the art world create a bottleneck for what is produced, and, consequently, what is accepted by audiences and critics.

This phenomenon of failure is replicated in all the arts. It is most notable in the theater because theater artists create in real time and in so doing, are the most vulnerable. Critical response to their artistry is immediate. Of all artists, theater people are most prone to panic when exposed to the toxin of failure. A bad review immediately affects the ability of the entire group to earn a living. Unlike film, there is no time to find new work before the old work is exposed; and unlike the world of art galleries, there is no gallery owner doing spin for a bad review. The theater artist lives and dies by the critic, and the money follows the critical response. Art is pressed into the service of pleasing critics, then backers, then the audience and, only lastly and forlornly, the artist.

We wondered what would happen if the capital threshold for creating art were lowered? What if, as in the case of the *Moose Murders* revival, we made a philosophy out of a do-it-yourself financing with absolutely no expectation of profit or advancing reputations? What if, amidst the debris of corporate financed art, the goal was to keep it simple and simply have fun? What if creating art in the twenty-first century happened on a playground rather than a minefield? What would the modern artist look like then?

Hard stuff to resist for *this* aging Adult Child of an Alcoholic, let me just say.

Hell, I was so starved for this kind of unconditional affection (even if it was just for my play), is it any wonder that I immediately agreed to give J. W. Borek not only the exclusive rights to carry out any or all of his nefarious Post Cap intentions on this play of mine, but also the right to add a full score by a (strangely brilliant) duo of local musicians—a score which, I am quick to add—at any given moment—may or may not be performed in tandem with the play or its plot?

I think not, Madame or Sir.

He was, as he insisted on calling himself as often and earnestly as possible, John W. Borek, *your producer*, and I saw no reason to doubt him whatsoever—especially when I learned that his tenacity and talent at self-promotion had attracted the attention of *Times* journalist Campbell Robertson, who now, I was told, was interested in writing a story about John and his "moosies." I was very nervous about taking an interview with this acclaimed Broadway reporter myself, not because I didn't like or crave the attention, certainly, but because I was terrified I was going to say something injuriously dorky and have it printed for everybody in all my past and present lives to see.

No matter what angle I tried to take as I practiced mentally for this interview, I couldn't shake the real fear that this was just another opportunity for somebody to poke fun at my literary deformity. Did I really want to exhibit myself *intentionally* in such a shameless manner?

As I told Campbell somewhere in the middle of our totally comfortable phone conversation—and I *love* this line because I've never once winced while reading it—*If you can't redeem, exploit.*"

And once I'd admitted that to myself, and owned up to the fact that redemption wasn't merely improbable but just not that *important* anymore, and that there was precious little left to be said about this ridiculous play I'd written over a quarter of a century ago that could puncture through the years and years of scar tissue, I relaxed enough not only to take the interview but actually have some fun with it.

And here I must give the lion's share of credit to Campbell, who put me at ease by treating me like an old friend he'd just run into at the Equity Lounge or something. The article itself, which appeared in April 2008 (a mere six months before John was to create his Post Cap Manifesto), was titled: "A Broadway Flop Again Raises Its Antlers."

"The cast," wrote Campbell, referring to the cast of "nonprofessional—most barely even amateur actors" involved in the Rochester Contemporary Art production, "included an antiques retailer, a culinary student, a muralist and a Spanish exchange student. They performed with scripts in hand, though some longer scenes were simply narrated. The mysterious moose character was a woman dressed in black holding an inflatable deer head emblazoned with the Miller High Life logo. Sidney Holloway, the mummified quadriplegic, was played by a mannequin, whose head rolled off during the first act. The audience members, most of them anyway, seemed to love it."

Please indulge me as I repeat that last line.

The audience members, most of them anyway, seemed to love it.

Now *there* was a comment about the Moose I'd never read before.

Campbell had also attended the cast party held at the L & M Bowling Lanes in downtown Rochester directly after the "anniversary performance" of John W. Borek's production of *Moose Murders* (A Moose-ical Renaissance). Karen, bubbling over with muse-ical joy, called me from these festivities, and managed to get the Man of the Hour to pick up the phone to say "hi."

"You really are Guffman," I said, referring to that Christopher Guest film about the exploits of an amateur theater company in Missouri. "What can I tell you? This was a lot of fun!" Campbell insisted, and, once I'd read his article a few weeks later, I began to take him at his lovely words. His piece in the *Times* became one of the most popular hits of the week (both off and online), and was quickly picked up by the *International Herald Tribune*. It spawned a few more articles in the (gasp!) *bring back Moose Murders* vein, including a gossipy blog item that admitted: "Reading Robertson's discussion of the show's epically awful notices — and reading Frank Rich's vicious Times review, which has helpfully been linked to the piece — made us nostalgic for a time when reviewers would trash a show without worrying about hurting anyone's feelings. ...surely we'll be seeing this new, ironic production of *Moose Murders* at the Fringe next summer, right? We can only hope so."

As a result of this miniature press blitz, I became an overnight celebrity at work (up to this point I'd managed to keep my identity safely hidden from most of my colleagues), and for a few madcap days my voice mail spilled over with some very intriguing blasts from the past.

"This was the first time," cooed one of my friends, "that I actually heard *your voice* in a story about Moose Murders. It's about time!"

In July—perhaps as a reward for his latest cutting edge work on the Moose—the *Times* reassigned Campbell to Baghdad as a "nontraditional" war correspondent. He seemed fine with this, and has done very well since, but I still think that this sudden move was a little on the (coincidentally) extreme side.

Anyway, if a smart, savvy, thoughtful writer from the *New York Times* actually had what he deemed *fun* at this reanimated version of my show, I thought, who was I to turn down an invitation to join the moosies in August for their gala New York City debut at Sardi's Eugenia Room?

Despite years of perfecting the art of total self-protection, I couldn't talk myself out of this one. It was time to return to the scene of my crime.

I decided to pamper myself as much as possible in preparation for this event. I booked myself at a fancy hotel in midtown Manhattan that several of my travel-savvy colleagues had stayed at and loved. I made sure that my two closest friends—Ted Enik and Diana Doussant—would be there to hold my hand every step of the way, and I sent private invitations to the performance to a handful of folks (including my brother Bruce) I thought would be blindly supportive no matter what happened.

John, himself a little stressed out, was nevertheless making a weekend out of this. Along with the Sardi's revival, he'd also reserved a field in

Central Park for a Sunday matinee. I had no idea what condition I'd be in after the first performance, so I hedged my bets by booking an early train out of the city first thing Sunday morning.

As soon as I checked into the hotel, the desk clerk upgraded me to a suite—which I took as a good omen. So good, in fact, I considered holing up in the hotel with my "people" until Sunday morning. So much was going on, maybe I wouldn't be missed.

But instead, I walked a couple blocks from the hotel on Saturday afternoon to join John, his wife Jackie, and all the "moosies" for a tour of the Eugene O'Neill Theatre, which was currently housing the rock musical *Spring Awakening*. We all screamed, hugged, jumped up and down, and continued to carry on like school children throughout the tour. All these guys were truly tickled to have me join them, and the feeling was perfectly mutual. Afterwards, they gathered their random stuffed animals and other set pieces along with their handmade glittering posters, and set off on a promotional parade through the theater district, while I went back to the hotel to write a curtain speech.

Not that anyone had asked me to, but something told me I wouldn't regret the effort.

A couple hours before the show, Ted and Diana met me at Joe Allen's, where we made sure our table gave us a decent view of the *Moose Murders* poster hanging over the bar. Afterwards, they flanked me on our walk to Sardi's, where I met my brother and a few other people on the street outside the restaurant. Somehow or other they all managed to get me up the stairs and into the Eugenia Room intact.

Most of the folks sitting in the folding chairs and mingling around the jerry-rigged stage for this evening's performance were friends, acquaintances, and followers of Borek. The few friends of mine I'd notified of this event had all shown up as well, and I found it fairly easy to talk with them about anything and everything except whatever it was we were about to see.

John had reserved us three chairs front row center, but that was the last place I wanted to sit. With some difficulty I made my way to the right of the performing platform and chose a seat almost directly behind a pillar. Ted and Diana dutifully followed, and wedged themselves in beside me. More than one person tried to convince us to move to a location with a better sight line, but I would have none of that. I had no idea how I was going to react to this revival, and I wanted to make sure whatever involuntary spasms I might experience during the performance would be well hidden from the crowd.

I was trying as hard as I could to be nothing more than an innocent spectator. My gut told me this would be my best chance for survival.

Borek, garbed in the black robes of a judge or a professor emeritus, wafted his way from the back of the room onto the platform, opened his arms to welcome us all to this ceremonial celebration of "anti-Broadway," and proceeded to regale us with stories of the company's outlandish plans to broaden their horizons in the future. There were knowing chuckles and smatterings of applause from the crowd; so far this was like a better-than-average meeting of the Knights of Columbus . . . or the Moose Club, I suppose. The quirkiness was undeniably there, but there was nothing at the beginning to warn us that we were collectively about to step into an alternate universe. John concluded his remarks by acknowledging my presence, and, much to my relief, did not ask me to join him on stage or even to stand up. A few heads turned to check me out, but my pillar did its job and I was safely hidden from most of these glances.

Next Anthony Lovenheim Irwin and Joe Fox-Boyd, the composers and lyricists doubling as Howie and Nelson respectively, struck up the opening chords of their "Welcome to the Wild Moose Lodge," a song inspired by the play's opening stage directions. We just couldn't do any better than "we are in the middle of one of this region's notoriously severe rainstorms," Joe noted in his program bio. This was the first and last musical number to make any reference to the play itself. "In the spirit of anti-Broadway," Borek would explain in a later interview, "these are not songs that advance the plot in any way."

The rest of the cast, all sitting on stage in an arc of stools from the beginning, joined in at will with various props and musical instruments. When the song was done, they set about reading their unmemorized lines from their loose-leaf notebooks, some more convincingly than others, all of them with insane enthusiasm. Nurse Dagmar and her fractured English, as played by the irrepressible and stunningly beautiful University of Rochester Spanish exchange student Maria Cordorba, was a huge hit, as was local culinary student Mike Bulger, who valiantly wrestled with the dual roles of Stinky and little Gay. You could barely understand a single word either of these two said, but that hardly mattered. This afternoon wasn't about coherency.

The stage directions, as read by Borek's wife, Jacqueline Levine, seemed to be going over especially well. What I was missing from my obstructed view on stage left was the placement of a stuffed deer on the other side of the stage whose mouth had been rigged to move puppetlike to Jackie's every word. The stuffed deer head was telling the tale, you see. I loved that concept when I found out about it, and was really sorry I'd been too chicken-shit to sit where I could see it happening.

It took several minutes for me to feel the full effect of what was actually going on at this ritualistic piece of community theater. The audience was having a ball. They were totally into this lunacy. My play, mind you, was only indirectly responsible for this merriment, and the more I came to understand this, the rosier things got for me. About fifteen minutes into the performance I burst out with my first solid belly laugh. John told me later that although he couldn't see me (I'd made sure of that), when he heard me lose it, he knew he and I were home free.

At the end of the play, each cast member reached behind his or her stool and pulled out a two-by-three-foot Plexiglas poster of my face—a portrait I'd had done at Sears especially for my Facebook profile. I'd called it "Facebick," and here were a dozen animated Facebicks bobbing up and down on stage while Richard Storms, the fellow who'd just played Joe Buffalo Dance, strolled through the audience like Santa handing out Facebick buttons from a large sack. It was a narcissist's wet dream, and I hardly waited for John to beckon to me before lumbering onto the stage to take part in this spectacle.

I'm not sure, but I suspect in my gut that this was the kind of stage farce I'd been trying to accomplish all along. This was all still very much a joke, yes, but an incredibly joyous one, and one that perfectly reflected that fine line I'd been straddling between fame and infamy. I was Norma Desmond descending the stairs for my final close-up, yes, maybe—but with the distinct advantage of still having all my marbles.

I caught John's eye only briefly before he disappeared into the background, preoccupied already with his next overly ambitious project.

That's the way it is with Borek, as we all must learn if we hope to follow.

So I stayed on stage and faced my fate without him, waiting patiently for the crowd to quiet down enough for me to deliver the speech I'd been rehearsing for twenty-five years.

"Hello, suckers, my name is Arthur…"

"Hello, Arthur!"

(I just *knew* they would all cooperate!)

"…and I wrote *Moose Murders!*"

Index

Photos indicated by **bold** page numbers.

"The Aba Daba Honeymoon" (song), 45
ABC (TV network), 46
Actors' Equity, 32, 35, 37, 41, 97
  Equity Lounge, 159
  Equity Principal Interview (cattle calls),
  35–37
Adams, Bret, 118, 119, 124, 127
Aelred (Benedictine brother), 65, 139, 140,
  141, 142, 145
Agnes of God (play), 32
Air France, 33, 59, 70, 117, 148, 152
Alberto VO5, 37
Alfred Hitchcock's Mystery Magazine, 92
American Ballet Theater, 8
American Conservatory Theater, 132
Anatomy of a Murder (film), 12, 17
Anderson, Loni, 133
Angels in America (play), 151
Arden, Eve, 9, 58, 72, **101**, **102**, **103**, 117,
  144. See also Holloway, Hedda (*in Moose
  Murders*)
    age concerns, 16–17, 58
    and alcohol, 93, 94, 124
    children of, 17, 128
    death of in 1990, 10
    expectation she would begin every
      show, 97
    June Gable's views on, 150
    in *Moose Murders*, 9, 13, 48
      attending New Year's and New Show
        party, 72, 74–76
      falling on stage, 112
      need to be replaced, 104, 122, 123–124,
        127–129
      news story on her return to Broadway,
        70
      at press brunch, 77–78
      at the previews, 108–109, 116, 119, 120
      problems with her work, 86–88,
        89, 90–91, 93–94, 95, 99, 110, 113,
        117–118, 120–121
      reading for the part, 45, 46
      at the rehearsals, 68, 81, 83, 85, 89–90,
        107, 113
      salary, 95
      suggesting script changes, 13–16,
        68–69, 70, 84, 90, 99
    as a quick-change vocal artist, 11–12

relationship with Arthur Bicknell, 14–17,
  18–19, 65, 68–69, 78, 79, 83–84, 85–86,
  94, 110, 119, 124–125
trip to China, 18
Aronson, Boris, 51
Arthur, Beatrice "Bea," 21, 46
Associated Press, 88
Atkins, Christopher, 76
Auberjonois, René, 78
Auntie Mame (film), 37, 121

Backer, Brian, 48
Back Stage (trade tabloid), 49
"A Bad Case of Broadway Blues" (Pauly), 146
Bahl, Jerry, 100
Baker, Tammy Faye, 40
Ballard, Kaye, 128
Barnes, Clive, 7, 136, 144, 147
Barrymore's restaurant, 84, 134
Bates, Norman (in *Psycho*), 53
Bean, Orson, 89
Belasco, David, 51, 52, 55
Belasco Theater, 51–52, 57, 61
Bell, Arthur, 147
Bennett Studio. See Michael Bennett Studio
Bergen, Polly, 123
Bernhard, Sandra, 150
Bernstein, Leonard, 26
The Best Little Whorehouse in Texas (play), 32
Bicknell, Arthur, **103**, **104**, **105**. See also
  Florzak, Dennis, living with Arthur
  Bicknell
    after the opening night performance,
      142–146
    after the preview, 117
    career after closing of *Moose Murders*, 152
    comments on early plays, 32–33. See
      also *Moose Murders* (Bicknell)
    "Facebick" picture, 163
    first interview for *Moose Murders*, 91–92
    as inspiration for Austin Frost in *Murder
      on Cue*, 42
    relationship, with Holland Taylor,
      134–135
    relationships, with Eve Arden, 14–17,
      18–19, 65, 68–69, 78, 79, 83–84, 85–86,
      94, 110, 119, 124–125
    work before *Moose Murders*
      for Air France, 33, 59, 70, 117, 148, 152
      for Leo Shull, 49

Bicknell, Bruce (brother), 38–39, 132, 141, 160
Bicknell, Bruce (nephew), 141
Bicknell, Harrison (brother), 141, 143
Bicknell, Jane (sister-in-law), 141
Big Moose Lake, 39, 96, 113. See also Wild Moose Lodge
Bihm, Jerry, 93, 94, 112, 113, 123
"Bishop of Broadway." See Shin, Everett
The Blue Lagoon (film), 76
Bobbi Boland (play), 7
Bob Hope Christmas Special (TV show), 88
Bombeck, Erma, 52
Booth theater, 50
Borek, John W., **105**, 153, 157–159, 160–161, 162, 163
Boynton, Philip (in *Our Miss Brooks*), 75
Brack, Freddie, 39
Breakfast at Tiffany's (play version), 95
Breakfast with Les and Bess (play), 53, 127, 129, 149
Brenner, Christopher, 54
Brighton Beach Memoirs (play), 33
"A Broadway Flop Again Raises Its Antlers" (Robertson), 159
Brooks, Connie (in *Our Miss Brooks*), 11
Bulger, Mike, 162
Burke, Billie, 16
"Butcher of Broadway." See Rich, Frank

Caesar, Sid, 141
Caldwell, Zoe, 21, 28
California Suite (play), 66
Candide (Broadway revival of), 40, 149–150
Carnegie Mellon University, 24, 26, 41, 43, 57, 63, 67
Carpenter, Carleton, 45, 58
Carson, Johnny, 14
Castevet, Minnie (in *Rosemary's Baby*), 73
Castle, Marc, 45, 76, 93, **105**, 134, 136, 150
    at auditions, 42, 43–44, 53–55, 60–61
    disappointment, 62–63, 97
    opening night, 141, 142
    play dedicated to, 42, 44, 97
The Caucasian Chalk Circle (play), 38
CBS (TV network), 31
Chandler, Jeff, 75
Channing, Margo (character in film *All About Eve*), 68
Chaplin (play), 81
Chapman, Mark David, 26
Chapter Two (play), 66
Charisse, Cyd, 47

Charles, Vera (in *Mame*), 46
Charter, Mary Ann (mother of Dennis Florzak), 98, 99–100, 107, 108, 139, 140, 141, 142, 145
Chia Pets™, 114
The Chinese Viewing Pavilion (play), 29
Churchill, Caryl, 36
Circle in the Square Theater, 31
Cleaver, June (in *Leave It to Beaver*), 48
Cliff (assistant stage manager), 90
Cloud Nine (Churchill), 36
Collins, Pat, 67, 93, 94, 113
Columbo (TV show)+, 58
Copeland, Joan, 47–48, 56, 107, 119, 121, 122, 127
Cordorba, Maria, 162
Corman, Roger, 12
Coward, Noel, 31
Crane, Marion (in *Psycho*), 53
Crawford, Christina (in *Mommie Dearest*), 18, 60
Crawford, Joan, 16, 17–18, 60, 88
    Joan Crawford doll, 78, 79
Crimes of the Heart (play), 32, 50–51
Cullen, Hugh Roy, 24
Curtain Up (restaurant), 145

Dabdoub, Jack, 60, 109, 140. See also Joe Buffalo Dance (in *Moose Murders*)
    after the closing, 145
    at the rehearsals, 112, 114
Dagmar. See Nurse Dagmar (in *Moose Murders*)
Dakota (apartment building), 26, 28, 71, 76, 117, 147
Dark Shadows (TV show), 45
Davis, Eddie, 29, 31, 50, 59, 61, 66, 118
Dean, James, 25
DeBaer, Jean, 53, 61
Dentinger, Jane, 42–43, 76–77, 95, 98, **105**, 132, 133, 134, 136, 147
    as author of *Murder on Cue*, 42, 63, 98–99, 109
    opening night, 141, 142, 144
Dentinger, Mary, 144
Desmond, Norma, 163
Deutsche Grammophon, 8
De Vil, Cruella (in *101 Dalmatians*), 95
The Dining Room (play), 67, 78, 149
Doubleday Crime Club, 99
Doussant, Diana, 160, 161
Dreyfuss, Richard, 148
Drummond, Alice, 82

Dunaway, Faye, 60

Edgar awards, 92
The Effect of Gamma Rays on Man-in-the-Moon Marigolds (play), 21
The Electric Company (PBS TV show), 38
Ellery Queen's Mystery Magazine, 91, 117
Encore! Encore! (TV show), 8
Enik, Ted, 160, 161
Entertainment Tonight (TV show), 90
Equity Lounge, 159
Equity Principal Interview (EPI) (cattle calls), 35–48
Esquire (magazine), 149
Eugene O'Neill theater, 50, 66, 93, 108–114, 145, 161
    opening night, 139–153
    rent needing to be paid during suspension, 122
Eugenia Room at Sardi's, 142, 160, 161–163
Evans, Scott, **101**, **102**. See also Holloway, Stinky (in *Moose Murders*)
    auditioning, 53–55, 60, 61, 62–63
    and Eve Arden, 72, 75, 83, 84, 85, 124
    before first preview, 109
    and Holland Taylor, 130
    at press brunch, 78
    at the rehearsals, 83, 84
Ewing, J. R. (in *Dallas*), 25
Extremities (play), 32

Facebook, 156–157, 163
Falk, Peter, 58
The Fall of the House of Usher (film), 18
Family (TV show), 21
Famous Monsters of Filmland (magazine), 12
Fawcett, Farrah, 7
Fay, Lauraine Holloway (in *Moose Murders*), 82, **101**, 112. See also Robertson, Lillie
    casting of, 27, 29, 36, 38
    costumes for, 96
Fay, Nelson (in *Moose Murders*), 14. See also Hormann, Nicholas
    casting of, 22–23, 27, 36, 58, 66, 67
        Dennis Florzak as understudy, 41, 45, 62–63, 79
        Eve Arden wanting changes in character, 68–69, 70, 99
        at the previews, 120
        in reanimated Borek version, 162
        relationships with females in play, 56, 82
        with Hedda Holloway, 47, 84
Feingold, Michael, 147

Female Trouble (film), 38
Fisher, Albert, 50, 76, 111, 142
Fisher, Ricka Kanter, 50, 69, 95–96, **103**, **104**, 117, 122, 130, 135, 147
    after the closing, 147
    during casting, 31, 33, 37, 43, 44, 46, 48, 54, 56, 58, 59, 61, 63, 66
    and Eve Arden, 87, 88, 93–94, 95, 100, 107, 118
    handling Arden's replacement, 121, 123, 124, 127
    and Force Ten Productions, 26, 27–29, 31, 144
    June Gable blaming for the fate of Moose Murders, 149–150
    New Year's and New Show Party at the Dakota, 71, 76
    and opening night, 142, 143
    and publicity, 67–68, 91–92, 109, 121, 128
    theater choice, 66
Fitzgerald, F. Scott, 155
Five Easy Pieces (film), 38
Florzak, Dennis, 59, 60–61, 78–79, 93, **102**, **103**, **105**, 109, 135, 149. See also Holloway, Sidney (in *Moose Murders*)
    as Arthur Bicknell's agent, 11, 42, 45, 62
    diagnosis of cancer and death of, 152, 155
    and Eve Arden, 12, 13, 14–15, 17–18, 88, 108–109, 112, 117–118
    interest in playing Nelson Fay or understudy, 27, 41, 45, 62, 63, 79
    and John Roach, 19, 45, 95–96
    living with Arthur Bicknell, 11, 30, 31–32, 42, 62–63, 65, 76–77, 85, 110–111, 122, 134, 136, 152
    New Year's and New Show Party at the Dakota, 71–72, 73, 74, 76
    and opening night, 139–140, 142, 143–144, 145
    playing Sidney Holloway, 62–63, 70, 97, 117
    at press brunch, 77, 78, 79
    quitting his day job, 59
    views about Moose Murders, 70, 85, 88–89, 113, 117, 122
Flynn, Errol, 91
Flynn, Sally, 76, **105**
Follies (play), 51
Fonzarelli, Arthur "Fonzie" (in *Happy Days*), 46
"Force Nine," 24
Force Ten Productions, Inc., 33, 66, 70, **104**, 115

costs of Moose Murders, 146
handling fall out on replacing Eve
Arden, 124
and John Roach, 23–25, 26, 29, 30, 149
Johnson-Liff terminating casting
contract, 30, 31
and Lillie Robertson, 24, 26, 27
and Ricka Kanter Fisher, 26, 27–29, 31,
144
Fox-Boyd, Joe, 162
Francine, Anne, 46, 47, 107, 127
Frost, Austin (in *Murder on Cue*), 42

Gable, June, 67, **102**, 121, 129, 137. See also
Keene, Snooks (in *Moose Murders*)
after the closing, 145
article in *Esquire*, 149–150
attending New Year's and New Show
party, 74, 75
auditioning, 40–41, 57–59
costumes for, 79, 133
network of friends, 121, 129, 137
at press brunch, 78
and the previews, 116, 120, 123, 124
at the rehearsals, 82, 89, 91, 108, 112,
113–114, 120
Gallagher, Helen, 46
Game of Redemption, 6
Garfunkel, Art, 76
Gelder, Principal, 5–6, 10
General Partners, 146
Gere, Richard, 70
Getz, John, 66
Giant (film), 25
Gibson, William, 66
Gill, Brendan, 91
Glenn (Eve Arden's agent), 12–13, 16, 46,
122
Gomez, Googie (in *The Ritz*), 40
Graubert, Judy, 38
Grease (film), 16
Grease 2 (film), 16
Green, Michael Linden, 54
Guest, Christopher, 159
Gussow, Mel, 29

Hackett, Buddy, 41
Hall, Grayson, 45
Happy Days (TV show), 46
Harper Valley PTA (TV show), 46
Hart, Roxanne, 148–149
Harvey, Arthur J. (uncle), 141, 143
Harvey, Emma (aunt), 141

HBO (TV network), 31
Heatherton, Joey, 82
Heidi Chronicles (play), 151
Hellman, Lillian, 98
Hell's Kitchen (original name for *Paradise
Alley*), 24
Hellzapoppin' (play), 84
Helmond, Katherine, 21, 22, 28
Henley, Beth, 50–51, 66
Henry, Suzanne "Sue," 41–42, 43, 63, 90–91,
97, 109, 112, 127, 142
Heppel, Alan, 139, 142–143
Herman, Jerry, 78
Hitchcock, Alfred, 81
Hobel, Mara, **101**, **102**. See also Holloway,
Gay (in *Moose Murders*)
attending New Year's and New Show
party, 74
auditioning, 17–18, 60–61
at the previews, 116
publicity for Moose Murders
making first radio spot, 98
press brunch, 78, 79
at the rehearsals, 83, 86, 91, 112, 114, 131
relationship with Holland Taylor, 131
Hoffman, Dustin, 28
Hoffman, Julia (in *Dark Shadows*), 45–46
Holloway, Gay (in *Moose Murders*), 97, **101**,
133. See also Hobel, Mara
in an amateur production years later,
156
casting of, 17–18, 27, 36, 41, 46–47, 61
at the previews, 116, 120, 121, 133
in reanimated Borek version, 162
Holloway, Hedda (in Moose Murders), 13,
101, 118. See also Arden, Eve; Taylor,
Holland
casting of, 21–22, 27, 28, 36, 39–40,
47–48, 127–129
Eve Arden chosen, 45, 46, 48
replacing Eve Arden, 107, 118–119,
122, 123–124, 127–129
character portrayal
by Eve Arden, 14–16, 69, 83–85, 116
by Holland Taylor, 129–130
costumes for, 96
Sue Henry standing in for Eve Arden,
127
Holloway, Sidney (in *Moose Murders*), 41,
62–63, 70, 85, 113, 117, 159. See also
Florzak, Dennis
Holloway, Stinky (in *Moose Murders*), **101**.
See also Evans, Scott

attraction to his mother, 13, 36, 60, 75, 130
casting of, 27, 36, 39–40, 41, 43–44, 48, 53–55, 60–61
Eve Arden wanting name change, 13–14, 69
at the previews, 116, 120
in reanimated Borek version, 162
Hormann, Nicholas, 67, **102**, 128, 129. See also Fay, Nelson (in *Moose Murders*)
after the closing, 149
missing events, 74, 78–79
at the previews, 115
at the rehearsals, 82, 85, 91, 112, 120
Houdina, Mary Jane, 91
The House of Blue Leaves (play), 22
Howard, Stuart, 33–34, 52, 53
as casting director, 27, 36–37, 38, 43, 44, 54, 61
and Eve Arden, 45, 46, 48
finding replacement for Eve Arden, 118, 127
and Joan Copeland, 47–48, 56
"How I Survived Moose Murders, the Biggest Broadway Bomb" (Gable), 149–150
Hudson Guild Theatre, 53, 127
Hunt, Betty Lee, 32, 73, 77, 94, 111, 123, 128
Hunt, Douglas, 8
Hunt/Pucci Associates, 32

"Icky" as possible name for "Stinky," 14, 69
"I erected a tent," **102**
Innaurato, Albert, 147
International Herald Tribune (newspaper), 160
Invasion of the Body Snatchers (film), 37
Irwin, Anthony Lovenheim, 162
Ithaca College, 42
Ivey, Dana, 38

Jacobs, Bernard, 146
Janes, Betsy, 104
"Jeepers Creepers" (song), 40, 52, 91, 115, 142
Joe Allen's restaurant, 95, 161
Joe Buffalo Dance (in *Moose Murders*), 27, 36, 39, 41, 51, 59, 60, 61, 83, 163. See also Dabdoub, Jack
Johanson, Robert, 143
Johnson, Geoff, 21, 26, 28, 29, 33, 40
Johnson, Joyce, 7
Johnson-Liff Associates (casting agents for *Moose Murders*), 21, 22, 26, 29, 30. See also

Johnson, Geoff; Liff, Vinnie; Zerman, Andy
Jones, Jeffrey, 36, 41, 66
Josie (in *A Moon for the Misbegotten*), 156

Kalcheim, Lee, 53
Kaufman, George S., 42
Kaye, Danny, 47
Keene, Howie (in *Moose Murders*), 62, 83, 85, 97, 142. See also Potter, Don; "The Singing Keenes" (in Moose Murders)
in an amateur production years later, 156
casting of, 22, 23, 27, 31, 36, 38, 45, 58, 61
at the previews, 115, 116
in reanimated Borek version, 162
Keene, Snooks (in *Moose Murders*), 15, 63, 91, 108, 115, 135, 142. See also Gable, June; "The Singing Keenes" (in *Moose Murders*)
attempts to recapture "essence" of, 108, 137
casting of, 22, 27, 31, 36, 38, 40–41, 43, 52, 58
costumes for, 79, 82
as *Everyman* in the play, 133
inspiration for, 42, 58
Kellerman, Sally, 36
Kellogg, Marjorie Bradley, 31–32, 73, 79, 93, 94, 95, 96, **102**, 113, 145
Kelly (play), 95
Kelly, Roz, 46
Kerr, Barbara, 108–109
Kirkus (magazine), 99

L & M Bowling Lanes in Rochester, NY, 159
Lamb's Theatre, 58
Lane, Nathan, 8
Langella, Frank, 148–149
Lebowitz, Fran, 42
Leibovitz, Annie, 141
Lennon, John, 26
Lennon, Sean, 26
Lenska, Rula, 36–37
Levine, Jacqueline "Jackie" (wife of John W. Borek), 161, 163
Libertini, Richard "Dick," 23, 36
Liff, Vinnie, 21, 26, 28, 30, 33, 40
Lindstrom, Pia, 144, 146
"Live at Five" (WNBC), 122
Longtime Companion (film), 24
Looney Tunes (cartoons), 11
Lorre, Peter, 12
Lou Grant (TV show), 28

Lucas, Craig, 24, 42
Lundie, Ken, 91, 93

Macintosh, Cameron, 32
Mame (play), 46
Marat/Sade (play), 136
Marchand, Nancy, 21, 28
Marry Me a Little (play), 42
Masque of the Red Death (film), 12
Matthews, Anderson"Andy," 41, 63, 120
Mayberry RFD (TV show), 16
McCullers, Carson, 147
McGee, Principal (in *Grease* and *Grease 2*), 16
McMartin, John, 28
McMillan, Lisa, **102**, 109. See also Nurse Dagmar (in *Moose Murders*)
    after the closing, 144, 149
    auditioning, 56–57, 61, 63
    costumes for, 79
    at press brunch, 78
    at the previews, 116
    at the rehearsals, 83, 91, 114
McNally, Terrence, 40
McTigue, Mary, 37, 39–40, 44, 46, 47, 48, 53, 54, 55–56, 60
Meara, Anne, 22, 23, 29–31, 36
    Medea (Euripides), 28
Merrily We Roll Along (Furth and Sondheim), 136
Michael Bennett Studio, 37, 39, 48, 52, 58
Mickey Mouse Club (TV show), 58
Midnight Cowboy (film), 46
A Midsummer Night's Dream (Shakespeare in the Park), 38
Mildred Pierce (film), 11, 16, 75, 78
Mildred Pierce (restaurant), 76, 88
Miles, Sylvia, 46
Miller, Ann, 42
Miller, Arthur, 47, 131
Miller High Life logo, 159
Minskoff rehearsal complex, 68, 81, 85, 90, 108
The Miracle Worker (play), 66
Mommie Dearest (film), 18, 60
Monday After the Miracle (play), 66
A Moon for the Misbegotten (play), 156
Moose Murders (A Moose-ical Renaissance) revival, 159
Moose Murders (Bicknell), 155
    aftermath for
        amateur productions of, 155–157
        as a"classic flop," 149

fallout after play failed, 6
foreign rights for in Istanbul, 150–151
John W. Borek production, 157–159, 161–163
"moosies,"105, 158, 160, 161
offer to do a musical version: Moose Murders, the Afterbirth, 150
Philippine production giving Rich credit for writing Moose Murders, 156
Rich review 11 years later, 151
casting of, 21–29, 49–50, 52–63. See also Howard, Stuart; Johnson-Liff Associates (casting agents for Moose Murders); names of individual characters, i.e., Holloway, Hedda, Fay, Nelson, Keene, Snooks, etc.; Pulvino & Howard (casting company); Theatre Now, Inc.
    callbacks, 44, 45, 50, 51, 52, 58
    Equity Principal Interview (cattle calls), 35–48
    having a star in the show, 9, 13, 29
    replacing Eve Arden, 107, 118–119, 122, 123–124, 127–129
choice of title, 7, 8
choosing theater for the production, 50, 66
closing of, 145–146
costume design, 67, 79, 95, 96, 111. See also Sullivan, John Carver
dedicated to Marc Castle, 42, 43, 97
financials for, 146
going straight to Broadway, 33
graphics for, 32. See also Wilson, Gahan
hiring specialty staff, 91
    choreographer. See Houdina, Mary Jane
    "fight master." See Shelton, Kent
    music director. See Lundie, Ken
importance of director to actors, 23, 28
lighting for, 67, 113. See also Collins, Pat
New Year's and New Show Party at the Dakota, 71–76
official opening date, 50
Opening night, 139–153
other works compared to, 7–8
previews, 50
    Eve Arden asking to postpone, 113
    previews after Holland Taylor joins cast, 132–137
    previews with Eve Arden in cast, 108–109, 115–118, 119, 120–121

suspended until replacement for Eve Arden found, 118, 122
problems with the last scene, 84, 118, 119, 121, 128, 131–132
publicity for, 16–17
effect of replacing Eve Arden, 119, 123–124, 128
Entertainment Tonight interviewing Eve Arden, 90
erection of marquee, 92–93
Eve Arden canceling "events," 94
first Bicknell interview, 91–92
Moose paraphernalia, 104
official logo, 101. See also Bahl, Jerry
picture call, 111
press brunch for, 77–79
press representative, 31, 73. See also Hunt, Betty Lee
radio spots, 90, 98, 107–108
Serino, Coyne, & Nappi handling advertising and PR, 67
theater posters, 67, 92–93
rehearsals
date starting, 68
at the Eugene O'Neill theater with Eve Arden starring, 110–114, 120
at the Eugene O'Neill theater with Holland Taylor starring, 129–131, 134, 135
at the Eugene O'Neill theater with Sue Henry standing in, 127
at Minskoff rehearsal complex, 68, 75–76, 81–100, 107–109
reviews of, 6, 92, 121, 136–137, 143, 144, 145, 147–148, 150, 157–158
Frank Rich's comments on, 7, 8, 33, 149, 151, 160
set designs for, 31, 73, 96, **102**, 111, 145. See also Kellogg, Marjorie Bradley
effect of the rain machine, 116
use of rain machine, 111, 116, 117, 130
"'Moose Murders' is murdered—Investors Are, Too" (Shull), 146
Moose Murders Limited Partnership, 24
"moosies," **105**, 158, 160, 161
Morris, Howard, 140–141
Moss, Larry, 42
The Mothers-in-Law (TV show), 128
"Murder in the Dark" (parlor game in *Moose Murders*), 60, 61
Murder on Cue (Dentinger), 42, 98–99
Murray, Peg, 107, 127
My Great Dead Sister (Bicknell), 22, 24, 42,
43, 44, 147, 157
Mystery Writers of America, 92

NBC (TV network), 8, 46
NBC Entertainment, 31
Newhart, Bob, 25
Newley, Anthony, 81
Newsweek (magazine), 146
New York Daily News (newspaper), 70, 123, 127, 136, 146–147
New York Law Journal, 8
New York Magazine, 136
New York Observer (newspaper), 8
New York Post (newspaper), 7, 123, 129, 136, 144
New York Times (newspaper), 7, 8, 29, 123, 149, 151, 158–160
Nichol, Peter, 148
Nicholson, Jack, 38
Night of the Living Dead (film), 120
Nine (play), 57, 59
No, No Nanette (revival), 46
Noises Off (play), 151
Nurse Dagmar (in *Moose Murders*), 62, **102**. See also McMillan, Lisa
casting of, 23, 27, 36–38, 48, 52–53, 55–57, 59, 61, 63
costume design for, 79, 111
at the previews, 115, 116
in reanimated Borek version, 162
at the rehearsals, 83, 91
Nye, Carrie, 23, 28

O'Haire, Patricia, 123, 127
O'Hare, Brad, 41, 45
O'Neill theater. See Eugene O'Neill theater
Ono, Yoko, 26
On Your Toes (play), 147
O'Rourke, Jocelyn (in *Murder on Cue*), 42
Our Miss Brooks (radio show), 11, 13, 75
"Our Time" (song), 136

Pacino, Al, 28
Page, Geraldine, 21
Pagnozzi, Amy, 123
Pal Joey (play), 47
Paradise Alley (film), 23–24
Parker, Dorothy, 42
Parsons, David, 8
Passion (Nichol), 148–149
Pauly, David, 146
"People" (song), 52
Pied Piper (play), 8

Pink Flamingos (film), 38
Playwrights Horizons, 67
Plymouth theater, 50
Post, Emily, 52
Post-Cap Movement, 155–158, 159
Potter, Don, **102**. See also Keene, Howie (in
  Moose Murders)
    auditioning, 58, 61
    at the rehearsals, 83, 85–86, 91, 112, 113,
    114
Powell, Jane, 127–128
The Practice (TV show), 10
Prelude to a Kiss (film), 24
Present Laughter (play), 31, 38
Price, Vincent, 12, 18
Prince, Hal, 40
Production Company (off-Broadway
  production house), 24, 28, 29, 31, 42
Prymate (play), 7–8
Pulvino & Howard (casting company), 33,
  35, 51. See also Howard, Stuart; Schecter,
  Amy

Raidy, William, 147
Rear Window (film), 81
Reed, Rex, 91, 142
René, Norman, 24–25, 50
Reubens, Paul "Pee Wee Herman," 150
Reynolds, Debbie, 45
Ricardo, Lucy, 42
Rich, Frank, 7, 8, 33, 81, 136, 147, 149, 151, 160
    a production giving Rich credit for *Moose
    Murders*, 156
Richards, Lloyd (character in film *All About
  Eve*), 68
Riedel, Michael, 7
The Ritz (play), 40
Roach, John, 50, 69, 88, 95, **103**, **104**, 121,
  134–135
    after the closing, 147–148, 149
    on choice of theater, 50, 66
    commissioning a Bicknell screenplay,
    148
    as director, 16, 30, 31
      after replacing Eve Arden, 130–131,
      133, 135, 137
      blocking of the play, 82
      canceling previews, 122
      casting the play, 27, 28–29, 30–31,
      37–38, 40, 41, 43, 47–48, 52, 55–57,
      58–59, 61–62, 63, 66–67
      considering extending previews, 88
      dealing with Eve Arden, 11, 65, 68, 69,

77, 83–84, 85, 87–88, 107–125
      failing to direct, 29, 112–113, 114, 115,
      133, 134–135
      opening night, 140, 142, 144
      on order of billing on play poster,
      67–68
      at press brunch, 77
      and previews, 117, 118, 122, 136
      at the rehearsals, 81–100, 119–120
      showing frustrations, 96, 99
    and Force Ten Productions, 23–25, 26,
    29, 30, 149
    hosting New Year's and New Show
    party, 71–76
    June Gable blaming for the fate of
    Moose Murders, 149–150
    Lillie Robertson's husband, 11
    meeting with Florzak on Bicknell's
    contract, 45
    on selecting the theater, 66
    as undisclosed producer, 77. See also
    Force Ten Productions, Inc.
Robertson, Campbell, 158–160
Robertson, Corbin, 146
Robertson, Lillie, **101**, **102**, 115, 129, 140,
  145. See also Fay, Lauraine Holloway (in
  Moose Murders)
    acting the role of prima donna, 109, 112,
    114–115
    churlishness, 130–131
    after the closing, 144, 145, 146, 148
    at auditions, 52, 54, 56, 59, 62
    cast as Lauraine Holloway Fay, 27, 29
    costumes for, 96
    and Eve Arden, 88, 95, 117, 118, 121
    and Force Ten Productions, 24, 26, 27
    hosting New Year's and New Show
    party, 71–76
    John Roach's wife, 11
    at the O'Neill theater, before first
    preview, 109
    and opening night, 140, 144
    at press brunch, 77
    question on billing for on play poster,
    67–68, 93
    at the rehearsals, 82, 108, 109, 112, 114
Roca, Octavio, 8
Rochester "Moosies," 105
Rock Follies (British TV show), 37
Rocky (film), 24
Rooney, Mickey, 84
Rosemary's Baby (film), 26, 71, 73, 74, 76
Russell, Roz (in *Auntie Mame*), 121

Saint Martin's College, 65

Sands, Paul, 23

Sardi's restaurant, 49–51, 92, **104**, 142–144, 147

    "moosies" and reanimated version of *Moose Murders*, 160, 161–163

Schecter, Amy, 33–34, 35–36, 38, 44, 47, 51, 52, 56–57

Scott, George C., 31

Serino, Coyne, & Nappi (advertising and PR), 67

Seven Brides for Seven Brothers (film), 128

Shaffer, Anthony, 147–148

Shay, Michelle, 38

Shelton, Kent, 91, 93

Shin, Everett, 51

Show Business (trade tabloid), 49, 146

Shubert Organization, 140, 146

Shull, Leo, 49, 50, 146

Shull, Richard B., 38

Simon, John, 136, 150

Simon, Neil, 66, 92

Simpson, Vera (in *Pal Joey*), 47

"The Singing Keenes" (in *Moose Murders*), 22, 31, 36, 91, **102**, 115. See also Keene, Howie (in *Moose Murders*); Keene, Snooks (in *Moose Murders*)

Smith, Alexis, 21, 28

Smith, Liz, 122, 128–129, 146–147, 150

Smith, Lois, 38

Snoopy!!! (play), 58

Solomon's Child (play), 28

"Something has gone terribly wrong" (first body discovered), **102**

Sondheim, Stephen, 42, 136

Sophie's Choice (film), 14

Spring Awakening (play), 161

Stage Door (film), 16

StageWest, 152

Stallone, Sylvester, 24

Stapleton, Jean, 21

"A Star is Shorn" (article in *New York Post*), 123

Star Ledger (newspaper), 147

Steaming (play), 32

Stein, Gertrude, 146

Stevens, Fisher, 48

Stewart, Jimmy, 81

Stiller, Jerry, 21–22, 30

Stole, Mink, 38

Stritch, Elaine, 123, 127

Studio Duplicating Services, 69

Studio One, 37

Sugar Babies (play), 84

Sullivan, John Carver, 67, 74, 78–79, 96, 111

Sunday Magazine of the *New York Times*, 151

Tap dancing in *Moose Murders*, 36, 46–47, 60, 91, 112, 156

Taylor, Holland, **104**, 140. See also Holloway, Hedda (in *Moose Murders*)

    after the closing, 10, 145, 148, 149

    auditioning for part of Nurse Dagmar, 48, 52–53

    at the rehearsals, 129, 130–131, 134, 135

    efforts to fix last scene, 131–132

    relationship with Arthur Bicknell, 134–135

    as replacement for Eve Arden, 127–129

Te Kanawa, Kiri, 8

That's Entertainment (film), 45

Theatre Now, Inc., 29, 31

Thompson, Sada, 21–22, 23, 36

Tony awards, 40, 42, 148, 149

Torch Song Trilogy (play), 32

Total Abandon (play), 33, 148, 149

The Train Ride to Hell (Bicknell), 5

Tryon, Tom, 99

Tuscadero, Pinky (in *Happy Days*), 46

Two by Two (play), 47

Two Weeks with Love (film), 45

"Uncle Goopy" (in parody of *This Is Your Life*), 141

Understudies, 61–62, 97. See also Florzak, Dennis; Henry, Suzanne "Sue"; O'Hare, Brad; Zerman, Andy

settling in at the O'Neill theater, 109

Upson, Claude (in *Auntie Mame*), 121

Upson, Gloria (in *Auntie Mame*), 37

Utamaro: The Musical (play), 8

Valley of the Dolls (film), 9

Vanities (play), 43

Vanity Fair (magazine), 9

Venuta, Benay, 17, 83

Village Voice (newspaper), 147

Waiting for Guffman (film), 159

The Wake of Jamie Foster (play), 50, 66

Walters, Barbara, 91

Washington Times (newspaper), 8

Wasserstein, Wendy, 136, 151

Waters, John, 38

Watt, Doug, 136, 147
Webber, Andrew Lloyd, 32
"Welcome to the Wild Moose Lodge"
 (song), 162
West, Brooks, 12, 13, 15, 16, 17, 18, 46,
 71–72, 75, 88, 90, 108–109, 111, 117, 120
West Side Story (operatic treatment of), 8
Whodunnit (play), 148
Wild Moose Lodge, 36, 73, **102**, 108, 111,
 131, 162. See also Big Moose Lake
Willis, Dean, 8
"Will Powell Go Straight?" (article in *New
 York Times Daily News*), 127
Wilson, August, 92
Wilson, Gahan, 32

Winer, Karen, 156, 157, 159
Winger, Debra, 70
Winkler, Irwin, 24
WNBC TV, 122
WNCN (radio), 98
Wolfe, Wendy, 52, 57
Woodhouse, Rosemary and Guy (in
 Rosemary's Baby), 26

Yale Drama School, 67
Youngman, Henny, 49

Zerman, Andy, 21, 26, 28, 30, 34, 109
at the rehearsals, 97
The Ziegfeld Follies (revival of), 16

20403637R00102

Made in the USA
Lexington, KY
02 February 2013